LIVING the Beatitudes TODAY

LIVING
the
Beatitudes
TODAY

Guy Robert Peel Steward

AMBASSADOR INTERNATIONAL
GREENVILLE, SOUTH CAROLINA & BELFAST, NORTHERN IRELAND

www.ambassador-international.com

Living the Beatitudes Today

ISBN: 978-1-64960-036-3
eISBN: 978-1-64960-037-0

Cover Design by Hannah Nichols
Interior Typesetting by Dentelle Design
Edited by Daphne Self

All Scripture references are from the King James (Authorised) Version

AMBASSADOR INTERNATIONAL
Emerald House
411 University Ridge, Suite B14
Greenville, SC 29601, USA
www.ambassador-international.com

AMBASSADOR BOOKS
The Mount
2 Woodstock Link
Belfast, BT6 8DD, Northern Ireland, UK
www.ambassadormedia.co.uk

The colophon is a trademark of Ambassador, a Christian publishing company.

Blessed *are* the poor in spirit: for theirs is the kingdom of heaven.

Blessed *are* they that mourn: for they shall be comforted.

Blessed *are* the meek: for they shall inherit the earth.

Blessed *are* they which do hunger and thirst after righteousness: for they shall be filled.

Blessed *are* the merciful: for they shall obtain mercy.

Blessed *are* the pure in heart: for they shall see God.

Blessed *are* the peacemakers: for they shall be called the children of God.

Blessed *are* they which are persecuted for righteousness' sake: for theirs is the kingdom of heaven.

Blessed are ye, when *men* shall revile you, and persecute *you,* and shall say all manner of evil against you falsely, for my sake.

Rejoice, and be exceeding glad: for great *is* your reward in heaven: for so persecuted they the prophets which were before you.

— Matthew 5:3-12

CONTENTS

FOREWORD

Living the Beatitudes Today is a refreshing look into the first part of Jesus's teaching on the mountain in Matthew's gospel. It shows how Jesus linked the central and permanent teachings of the Old Testament with His own teaching and ministry. These beautiful truths are the bedrock for His followers for all time.

Those on the journey of faith have always and must always start from a position of recognising their own need. They must have a God-given desire to follow God and by so doing seek peace for those around them. Even in the face of persecution and opposition their faith remains.

Living the Beatitudes Today reminds us that need and hardship can be signs that God is at work amongst us. The life of Jesus Himself shows us this. His physical poverty, social rejection and violent death were means by which He would draw near to His Father and depend on His promises. In our weakness and struggles we too can be strong as we lean more on the sufficiency of God..

Each discussion on the Beatitudes begins with common contemporary objections to what is being taught. The teachings now, as they were when first delivered, challenge us to see things with the eyes of faith. Sorrows become joys in the light of God's faithful love. You will be blessed by meditating on these timeless truths.

JONATHAN DOVE
Senior Pastor
Gracecity Church

PREFACE

In this book I use the work of the experts for my linguistic source material and reference, i.e., W.E. Vine's *An Expository Dictionary of New Testament Words* and *Strong's Concordance*. Jesus spoke Aramaic (the lingua franca in Galilee), Hebrew, and at least some Greek, which was the wider lingua franca used in the Roman world since the time of Alexander the Great. There is no exact transcript of His original words in any of those languages apart from a few Aramaic references (e.g., *Abba* – "father", *Raca* – "fool, vain fellow", *Talitha Cumi* – "Damsel, I say unto thee, arise"). The New Testament writers used all three during the first century A.D., and it is probable that the earliest—possibly draft—notes of Matthew were in Hebrew. The poetic nature of the original Scriptures has been translated well enough into English in the Authorised Version, and it is quite reasonable to argue that little has been lost in translation. Semitisms create some difficulties at times, but much is plain to see with a small amount of study. From this standpoint, the Authorised Version is used in this book with little reference to other versions or paraphrases.

INTRODUCTION

Two thousand years ago, as the sun rose over the Lake of Galilee in the land of Israel, a man named Jehoshua (the Hebrew word for "Jesus") arose from His night's sleep—or perhaps from a whole night in prayer—and began His morning devotions. He prayed that on that day God would open His closest followers' spiritual ears and eyes so that they might fully understand what He was about to tell them.

Not long before this, He had declared His life's purpose in a synagogue at His own hometown of Nazareth near the Lake (also referred to as "sea") of Galilee. He had learned that "A prophet is not without honour, but in his own country, and among his own kin, and in his own house" (Mark 6:4). His declaration of purpose about healing broken-hearted people, preaching freedom to captives, bringing sight to the blind and liberty to those bound up by the hurts and wounds of life had not been well-received. Thus, it was clearly a good time to move on from there and to the little town of Capernaum at the northern end of the Sea of Galilee. It was good for Him to go somewhere quiet where He could continue His ministry.

The day in question was to be a special day, though His followers were unaware of its significance beforehand. He was about to give His first didactic (instructional) talk to His disciples. He may have considered how He would start His talk that day, knowing that it would be recorded forever in what would eventually become Holy Scripture, on a level with the hallowed law of Moses. The idea may have come to Jesus that morning, perhaps the night before, perhaps even in His spirit years before—and divinely ordained—that *this* revelation would not only support the law of Moses, but would actually fulfil it in a powerful new way.

He may have been thinking about the very last word of the Torah—the revered holy Scriptures of the ancient nation of Israel—written by the prophet Malachi some four hundred years before.[1] The word was "curse". He may have thought about how Malachi had, in his final thoughts, quoted God saying, "Remember ye the law of Moses my servant, which I commanded unto him in Horeb [Sinai] for all Israel, *with* the statutes and judgments" (4:4). Malachi had then warned that the earth would be cursed if the hearts of the fathers and the hearts of the children were not reconciled to each other. The fifth commandment was the pivotal hinge between the first four commandments and the last five; its command was simple: to honour your father and mother. It's significance, however, was complex. Five is the biblical number of redemption, of grace, of "turning back", of reconciliation—the *hei* (ה) or breath of God in the Hebrew alphabet. Further, (although all commandments obeyed would bring blessing), this was the only commandment that came with a specific promise of a blessing if it was obeyed. That blessing was "that thy days may be prolonged, and that it may go well with thee" (Deuteronomy 5:16).

Whereas the Hebrew Scriptures had finished with a word which denoted images of failure, of disaster, of judgement, of a *curse,* this new word would start with its direct opposite—a blessing. Thus the words, we can imagine, came to Jesus—"blessing", "bless", *"blessed!"*,*"blessed* are those who".

This was a message from eternity to every human, but for now, it was to His own inner circle. Jesus was about to initiate a movement that would only be completely fulfilled in the far distant future, but would start to change the entire world only a few years from then. In fact, it had already begun.

God did not want to curse, but to bless, and it was the blessing of reconciliation.

---

1   Malachi was the last of the prophetic books in the Hebrew Bible.

ORIGINS OF THE BEATITUDES

So, where did this message come from? Were there any precedents in previous writings? Were there really "caring" communities practising these laws in the centuries and millennia prior to the giving of the Beatitudes? It is evident that the second half of the Ten Commandments dealt specifically with certain laws which, when followed, had the capacity to help societies and individuals to be compassionate and considerate of others, as well as to honour the God who gave them. All those commandments were codified expressions of what had been "breathed" into the human conscience from the beginning by the Creator, and are illustrated in the Scriptures prior to the revelation at Mt. Sinai. They were evident in the consciences and actions of the various characters in the book of Genesis, either in how they followed them or in how they broke them. God's reprimands and dealings with these people reflected His call for moral integrity, which was then communicated in an ordered fashion and developed as basic principles in the books of Moses—Exodus, Leviticus, Numbers, and Deuteronomy. There, the various laws were clearly, logically, and systematically laid out in a legal way, while also being interspersed with theological and historical matters.

In that earlier revelation, there were two types of commandment given:

1) Casuistic – in which a commandment is given with a consequence, "such and such a penalty will be applied to whoever does that wrong thing," often written in the conditional, i.e., "*if* anyone does that . . . then *this* will be the consequence", and

2) Apodictic – or absolute, where it is a case of "don't do this" or "do this", but with no punishment stated.

Although the basics of these laws of Israel (with exception for the ceremonial/ritual/sacrificial laws) can be found to some degree in the human psyche, the written revelation was necessary for there to be any absolute sense to them. Ultimately, that revelation was not just meant to be for a particular tribal group. Consequently, the morals and ethics implied by them apply today everywhere, regardless of the tenor of social beliefs. The tenth commandment, for example, goes to the heart of the problem of sin and is relevant to any society. While casuistic stoning laws were abrogated by Jesus's teachings, they originally revealed the seriousness of law transgression and the holiness of the law. The *application* of moral laws, such as those that deal with the value of human life, is a reality still in process in every society.

Here in the Beatitudes, we are reminded of both casuistic and apodictic law in a completely positive way—there are no "thou shalt not's" here or even "thou shalt's"—yet they are all implied. For example, if you are merciful, or righteous, or a peacemaker, it follows that you will not commit murder, or harm anyone, or commit any type of deliberate offence to anyone.

Here also, in what appears to be Jesus's foundational address, there is a powerful refinement of the law that was in the Torah (the Old Testament). While almost all of the Beatitudes can be found (some virtually verbatim), in various parts of the older revelation, only here in Matthew's gospel are they laid out plainly, systematically, and concisely, and this may be the very reason why Jesus felt the need to repeat them. Not only were they timely but also here in His first recorded teaching was the opportunity to put them all together in a pithy, punchy discourse where the listeners could grasp what He was saying immediately.

Most listeners in Jesus's time were not particularly literate or scholastic in the modern sense, which is why Jesus had to say at times, "Ye have heard that it hath been said". For many of them, they had *only* heard because they did not or could not read, at least not regularly, though of course there would have been some exceptions. It was "said" because the Word of God in the past had been "said" by God and subsequently "said" by Levitical scribes and rabbis. The latter had also added orally to the whole collection of obligations as in their practise of tithing of mint and anise, but in this first part of His discourse, after many centuries of "silence" in the prophetic area of the religion, Jesus gave a basic summary of the law in just nine statements, each one a deep treasure. For us to get the meanings clear today, it is necessary to dig a bit further.

The whole Sermon on the Mount, as found in chapters five, six, and seven of the book of Matthew, has been called the greatest speech and the most powerful discourse on correct human relations and religious behaviour ever given. It is as worthy of our attention as are the Ten Commandments! The Beatitudes, which form its introduction, hearken back to, and show the perfection of, the ancient law, especially in human relationships, but they are also for today, and speak prophetically of how things will one day be in the future. Impossible in one sense for us to keep in the natural, they require a greater power than we can summon up ourselves—the power of Jesus Christ.

THE SIGNIFICANCE OF THE MOUNTAIN

God gave some of His greatest revelations on mountains. Abraham was on Mt. Moriah when he encountered the voice and the intervention of God, and Moses was on Mt. Sinai when he received the Commandments.

They are also sometimes places of battle and victory. The Old Testament prophet Elijah successfully confronted the prophets of Baal on Mt. Carmel, and Jesus overcame the devil's offer of the kingdoms of this world on a high mountain. For at least some of the Sermon on the Mount[2], a revelation as significant as that given to Abraham or Moses, Jesus was on a hill in Galilee. On

---

2   The foothills of Galilee are near the northern plain, and in Luke's gospel it is stated that either the same or a similar type of discourse was conducted "on a plain", meaning, "a level place", which was also where He did some of his preceding ministry (Luke 6:17-19). Luke's account could have been located at a level place on Matthew's "mountain" (no one knows exactly where this was) or perhaps somewhere different, and hence, a different address to a different audience (though still in the vicinity of Capernaum and Galilee). There are similarities, and some passages are virtually the same, but there are also differences. Luke, for example, only includes four Beatitudes and then adds four "woes", reminiscent of previous prophetic utterances as found in Jeremiah, Isaiah, and Ezekiel, while Matthew has eight Beatitudes, or nine if the last is divided into two. Even if it was a different time and place, the two passages may be compared, even harmonised to a degree, to illustrate the thrust of Jesus's overall message. It is possible that the Sermon was taught on other occasions or even over a period of time. It could be a collection of sermonettes, expertly arranged by the writer with the main content delivered on the occasion that Matthew depicts here and starting with the Beatitudes. It does seem though that it has come to us with both a beginning (Matthew 5:2) and an ending (Matthew 7:28); so, either what we have is everything He said, or else it is a briefer version of a longer dissertation. Someone present then or on any of the sermonette occasions (if that was the case) would have taken notes, later to be organised into what we have now in these chapters.

this hill or mountain, Jesus's disciples came to Him. He had already called for repentance and given the invitation to "Follow me, and I will make you fishers of men" (Matthew 4:19). He had already taught in the synagogues (places of worship), in one of which He had declared His whole purpose by preaching the gospel of the kingdom (Luke 4:18) as mentioned above, and had already healed "all manner of sickness and all manner of disease" amongst the people. His fame had gone out over "all Syria", north of Galilee. He had healed those with "divers diseases" as well as "those which were possessed with devils, and those which were lunatick" (Matthew 4:23-24). Many today testify that He still carries this power to heal bodily as well as psychological, emotional, and spiritual ills.

Back then, a host of people had come from Galilee, Decapolis, Jerusalem, Judæa, and beyond Jordan—a very widespread area. "Seeing the multitudes" got Jesus started on the job of training His disciples, as after His parting, they would be the ones to continue His ministry. (Perhaps Jesus was foreseeing the multitudes who would be touched down through the centuries by the very words He was about to say.)

On this particular occasion, He had the urge to go up a mountain and settle. It says "when He was set", which meant He was seated, but also figuratively "settled", as if to have a rest. His own peaceful presence would probably have caused His disciples also to be settled and relaxed, and to listen attentively, and thus to be in a teachable place. Jesus knew that that's where people learn deep truths best, when they are unflustered, unhurried, and rested. This was time out from the busyness of His ministry, and, for His listeners, from the bustle of their daily activities and work. We can imagine His eyes compassionately scanning the faces of His audience as He waited for them to quieten down and to focus on Him. His opening words—these Beatitudes—would have then come clear and resonant as He spoke, and were intended to echo down through all time, never losing their impact and significance. There must have been a great sense of anticipation as they sat there, waiting to hear what He would say. "He opened his mouth", and when

He spoke, they listened; surely, no words were wasted. It is generally accepted that this discourse was intended for all of His followers from then on.

There is so much that we cannot know about this part of "the Sermon on the Mount". We do not know what time of day it was—whether it was morning, evening, or midday, though it was perhaps more likely to be the morning.

We don't know what the temperature was—whether it was cold, hot, or mild.

We don't know what the weather was like—sunny, overcast, with a breeze, or maybe a few drops of rain.

We don't know what the area smelled like—perhaps the fresh air of a higher altitude, maybe the fragrance of flowers and trees, or the smell of cooking from habitations lower down the hill.

We don't know how the people were seated, or what they were sitting on.

We don't know how many people were there.

We don't know what Jesus's voice was like, or how long He took to give His address.

We don't know if he stood at some point and moved around during His teaching. It was the custom then for rabbis to sit and Matthew's use of "set" affirms this. John's gospel, in a passage possibly referring to the same event (6:3), states "there he sat", while in Luke's "plain sermon" He is standing.

All we know is that it happened on a hill in Galilee two thousand years ago.

What then of the writer Matthew?[3] As a former tax collector, he had been in a then-despised career that sometimes involved corruption as well as disloyalty to Israel because of his obligations to the Romans. As a result, he would have been rejected from certain aspects of society, including attendance at the synagogue. There was social stigma attached to his profession. Though he had turned his back on mammon after his momentous meeting with the

---

3   All the writers of all the four gospels are anonymous; however, the names attached to them are accepted by tradition and scholastic opinion as being the most likely writers. It would seem that in those days, it was either not the tradition or else inappropriate for them to add their name. Assuming that this writer actually was the disciple Matthew, we can gain some insight into his thinking by considering his former occupation.

Messiah, it is evident that he was still a wealthy man since he hosted "a great company of publicans" in his house (Luke 5:29). It could have been seen then as somewhat condescending for him to write, "Blessed are you poor", in the early part of his gospel; so, unlike the physician Luke, who *did* write "poor" (and actually gave more focus to the poor in his gospel), Matthew writes, "Blessed *are* the poor in spirit", which seems to imply a different thing from simply being poor. Jesus taught on the subject of the "poor" as well as the "poor in spirit". In fact, all these nine Beatitudes are contrary to Matthew's former profession as a tax collector and to his old life in that capacity, so the change of mind and heart is further confirmed to a first-time reader by these words about poverty of spirit. Here, the "reject"—the reformed tax-collector—embraces his true heritage and from the outset, quotes the Master's words in the tradition of the prophets of Israel, showing that all these traits were now to be also his *own* desire and experience.

Up until now and for a few more verses, Jesus continues to speak very simply. It is usual for prophetic speakers in the Bible to write or be quoted in language which includes such literary devices as parallelisms, simile, allegory, metaphor, and hyperbole[4]. In contrast, the Beatitudes could not

---

4   Parallelisms are ways of emphasising a point. Different types are: synonymous, where the first line is echoed by the second but with different words, as in Psalm 2:3 or 6:1; synthetical, where there is a cause and an effect, the second idea building on the first, as in Isaiah 5:7; antithetical, where the first idea is affirmed by a contrasting second idea, as in Proverbs 14:30; and climactic/ascending where the first line is completed by the subsequent line/s, as in Psalm 1:1, Ezekiel 13:22, and Joel 1:4. All these are found throughout Scripture in both Old and New Testaments. Simile is when two things have a similarity, as in Habakkuk 2:14 ("knowledge of the glory of the LORD, as the waters cover the sea"). Allegory is when something stands as a figure of something else, as in Isaiah 5:1-7 ("vine" = Israel). Metaphor is when something is represented directly by another, as in Proverbs 7:2 ("the apple of thine eye") and Isaiah 4:2 ("the branch of the LORD"). Hyperbole is the use of exaggeration to drive home a point, as in Luke 18:25 ("a camel to go through a needle's eye"). Jesus (speaking in Aramaic or perhaps Hebrew) used these in many similar instances as the latter, another example being Matthew 11:28-30 ("Come unto me all ye that labour and are heavy laden."), a metaphor which when translated from the written Greek back into Palestinian Aramaic, "exhibits not only poetical structure, but also alliteration and even rhyme, and shows . . . that the model our Lord chose for His addresses was the poetical 'sermon' of the Hebrew prophets." ("The Language of the New Testament", by David J. A. Clines, *A New Testament Commentary*, Gen.Ed. G. C. D. Howley, 1969, p. 32.)

be more simple and plain. They are a statement of what we are to be and what will be the result of it. This is deliberate though, so that we can get the point without too much thought or analysis. Remember that they are both a link to all that has gone before in the Word of God *and* an introduction to Jesus's whole body of teaching and of ministry in which He exemplifies the Beatitudes and fulfils them perfectly through His own sinless humanity and divinity.

While the Sermon on the Mount was a teaching discourse addressed to Jesus's disciples, others appear to have been present or at least watching, hence here and throughout His ministry He was following God's pattern of teaching as per Isaiah 28:10: "precept upon precept, . . . line upon line, . . . here a little, *and* there a little". However, this was to be one of His meatiest sermons—three chapters full of precept upon precept and line upon line. His first recorded address to the world—His "inaugural speech", if you will—revealed the spirit of everything He would do and teach over the next three years, and it was all ultimately about blessing for the nation of Israel and for all who followed Him.

"Blessed" in Greek is *makarios,* the root being *mak,* meaning large or lengthy. The term *makros* means long, and the English prefix "macro" is derived from this. *Makarios* is found elsewhere, including seven times in the book of Revelation where it describes the "blessed":

1. " . . . he that readeth, and they that hear the words of this prophecy and keep those things which are written therein" (1:3)
2. " . . . the dead which die in the Lord from henceforth" (14:13)
3. " . . . he that watcheth,and keepeth his garments" (16:15)
4. " . . . they which are called unto the marriage supper of the Lamb" (19:9)
5. " . . . he that hath part in the first resurrection", (20:6)

and in the final references

6. Who "keepeth the sayings of the prophecy of this book" (22:7); and
7. Who "do his commandments" (22:14)

There are other places where blessedness begins the discourse or text, for example in the Psalms:

> "Blessed *is* the man that walketh not in the counsel of the ungodly". (Psalm 1:1)

> "Blessed *is he whose* transgression *is* forgiven". (Psalm 32:1)

> "Blessed *is* he that considereth the poor". (Psalm 41:1)

> "Blessed *are* the undefiled in the way, who walk in the law of the LORD". (Psalm 119:1)

> "Blessed *is* everyone that feareth the LORD; that walketh in his ways". (Psalm 128:1)

In each of these five cases, the Hebrew word *'escher'* is used, meaning "blessed, happy, happiness", but used as an interjection: "How happy!". It is also derived from a primary root meaning "to be straight, level, right, happy" and therefore figuratively "to go forward, be honest, prosper".

The Beatitudes hold similar promises of blessing, and Jesus used similar language in His use of "blessed", which is why some translations have rendered it as "How happy are they who". However, the English word "happy" does not on its own do the full meaning justice. There is so much more to the word "blessed", as seen in the promises that accompany each beatitude.

Finally, the Beatitudes are not just for some far off future date, but for now, and if this was not the case, then the whole passage would be largely meaningless, irrelevant, and unworthy of our attention. On the contrary, it is totally relevant for any person or any society at any time.

HOW TO READ THIS BOOK

At the start of each chapter of this book, there is an imaginary oppositional argument from a fictitious challenger who tries to state why that beatitude is irrelevant. This is called the *Objection*. To each *Objection*, there is a counter-argument or *Response,* which is also a preview of the rest of the chapter.

For purposes of memorisation, the whole biblical passage could be divided into threes, including the variation of the eighth into the ninth (the "you" ones) to complete the final triplet.

Hence:

> The first – poverty of spirit, mourning, and meekness

> The second – hungering and thirsting for righteousness, mercy, and pureness of heart

> The third – peacemaking, plus two slightly differing references to persecution

The promises start and end with promises of, firstly, the "kingdom of heaven" and lastly, a personal assurance of a "reward in heaven". They provide for us a beautiful transition from the Old Covenant into the New, a natural link easing us from one to the other. They are both an introduction to the new and a summary of all that was good and necessary in the old. And they remain a challenge for all followers of God from Jesus's day until now—and will be as long as the world endures. This book is written to prompt you to make a personal response, as well as to attempt to plumb the depths of these nine brief, but powerful statements. What do they really mean for us? What will they mean for you after you have understood them more clearly? And how can they become a reality in your life? I encourage you to read them through prayerfully first, and then, from the following chapters, to take the time to look at each one in greater depth, all the while considering their application.

POOR IN SPIRIT

"Blessed are the poor in spirit: for theirs is the kingdom of heaven."

Objection: *"Why should anyone be poor at all, let alone poor in spirit? The gospel of Luke just uses the word 'poor' . . . so who wants to be poor? We're all trying to be well-off, wealthy, or at least comfortable. Look at the poor in the world today. Are they really blessed? Are they happy? What does this 'poor in spirit' mean anyway?"*

Response: Spiritual "poverty" is not a reference to physical poverty. It can be compared to physical poverty only in the sense that the poor are generally not characterised by the self-satisfaction and conceit common to many of the rich. Also, the genuinely poor must frequently rely on the mercy of others to survive, just as believers have to learn to rely on God. Spiritual "poverty" can be seen though as a prerequisite for spiritual blessing. The recognition of our spiritual poverty, though often born out of despair, is the way to connect with God. Jesus's intention is never to leave us in absolute poverty of any kind forever, but to lift us up and out of it as we come to a place of spiritual dependence on Him as well as a place of personal humility.

In this first statement that formed the opening of Jesus's teaching to His disciples that day, we are confronted with something that goes against our natural desires to be comfortable or wealthy. Poverty of any kind is unwelcome in our lives, but what is this poverty "of spirit" and what could it mean? Why should we desire to have it?

Firstly, the initial three beatitudes are not talking about various groups of people—some poor, some mourning, and others who are meek. Rather, it's the one and the same experience that *all* can have to receive blessing. However, there are different aspects to it, and this is the first. Poverty of spirit is seen through the Bible as the key to entering into "the kingdom of heaven"—a kingdom that extends to earth. For example, when a person is "born again" on earth, they are ushered into the experience of heaven on earth. Heaven enters into their heart. So, if poverty of spirit is the key, it is evident that those without it are also *outside* the kingdom.

Poverty of spirit requires repentance.

The poor in spirit are the poor *of* spirit. In one sense, it is true that we are all poor of spirit since we all carry sin and failure, but only acknowledgement of this, along with honest contrition and repentance, can invite God's presence, thus meeting our spiritual poverty and giving us the riches of the kingdom. There is no heaven without a humble and contrite heart, so the "poor in spirit" experience is required for blessing.[5]

So what is it, this poverty of spirit? The word used for "poor" here is the same used throughout the New Testament, coming from the root *ptossō*, meaning "to crouch" as with a cringing beggar or pauper. The word for "spirit" is *pneuma,* meaning "breath/vital principle of life". The statement can now be contextualised to reveal more of what it means to be "a pauper or beggar for the breath of life or the vital principle of life".

Are there examples in the Bible of this? There are many: Abraham, Joseph, Job, Hannah (mother of Samuel the prophet), King David, Saul who became Paul in the New Testament, and others. These "begged", not as mendicant vagabonds in the street looking for money or food, but earnestly desiring God's dispensation of this "vital principle of life", i.e., life eternal and

---

5   See 2 Chronicles 34:27 for an example of this.

life abundant, and it came in each instance after a time of contrition and humbling. This is poverty of spirit.

"Be afflicted . . . and weep . . . Humble yourselves in the sight of the Lord, and he shall lift you up" (James 4:9-10).

What is a real beggar? He or she is someone who is *desperate for relief, and longing to be instated into a better condition.* A real beggar is one who has no other options. Perhaps only a certain percentage of beggars are genuinely so. Some are bogus and in their condition for ulterior purposes, or are so because of various vices or just plain lethargy; others are born into it with a background of families in dire circumstances, or are the way they are due to past choices. The beggars we are talking about in this illustration *want* to be free if given half a chance and don't want to have to beg. Apart from cases where they have become so accustomed to it that they *prefer* their beggarly existence to anything else, such people once set free of their condition will *never*—under any circumstances—willingly return to it. This is how *we* are to be with God, but we will never get there if we do not outwardly recognise our inward beggarly condition. Though we all have this ailment—many do not, or will not, acknowledge it. But just passively accepting it is still not enough. The remedy must be actively sought after. To be desperate for relief from sin, to have a longing to be saved from wretchedness, and a yearning for a better and more prosperous spiritual condition . . . *that* is what God honours, with the saving grace that ushers us in our hearts into His kingdom.

This poses the question: should we stay in a state of poverty of spirit after coming to God? The answer is as long as we are in our physical bodies, we will always be needing God's saving grace. The doctrine of total depravity does not teach that we all go around with wild-eyed, demented looks on our faces just waiting to do something evil. Rather, it just means that we are always in need of God's grace because we are never completely free from the pull of our sinful nature. Yet for the believer, God's grace constantly mitigates against our sinfulness, alleviating and diminishing its power. We can also grow to become more and more godly in our life and speech as we constantly walk in the light of God's grace, power, and love.

So, the initial phase of our conversion is like a baptism. Indeed, the physical act of baptism (a symbol of the death of our self-life which tries to enrich itself apart from God) illustrates it. From then on, it is a way of life. Poverty of spirit becomes an awareness of our dependency on the Divine— and in this sense, it is always to be with us, renewed and refreshed by our daily devotions, our daily "washing" or "baptism" which comes from our meditation on the Word of God (John 15:3; Ephesians 5:26; Psalm 119:97).

EXAMPLES FROM SCRIPTURE

Luke 16 speaks of a real beggar named Lazarus, and Luke 18 tells us that "a certain blind man sat by the wayside begging." Mark 10 identifies him as "blind Bartimaeus", and Jesus responded to his desperation. But there are many other examples in Scripture of the "poverty of spirit" described here—people desperate for relief and longing to be saved and appointed into a better and improved condition.[6] All exemplify this beatitude.

Poverty of spirit is what the Old Testament prophets pleaded with Israel for.

In the New Testament, Jesus described a man who in contrast to the self-righteous giver of alms in the temple, cried out, "God be merciful to me a sinner". This is poverty of spirit! He was justified and connected to the kingdom of heaven through the mercy of the King of kings, more than the self-righteous Pharisee (Luke 18:10-14).

Peter, the disciple of Jesus, came to a place of being "poor in spirit" when he "went out, and wept bitterly" after denying Jesus three times (Matthew 26:69-75). This also illustrates the second beatitude. Jesus had already said that Peter would deny Him three times that same night. To this, Peter was

---

6   See Ezra 8:21; 10:1, 6; Isaiah 6:5; Daniel 10:7-21; Acts 9:1-22; Acts 16:27-34 (the keeper of the prison).

indignant, sure that he would never do such a thing. Yet it happened while he was waiting outside the palace where Jesus was being tried. He was questioned by a couple of "maids" (including one of the high priest's) and "those that stood by". His denials got more intense each time, the first being a plain denial, the second with an oath, and the third with cursing and swearing. Then, the cock crowed, and Jesus looked at him from afar off. In that moment, Peter was totally undone—and from then on, he was a different man and went on to become a pillar of the early church. He was given "the kingdom of heaven" as he served the Lord and followed his commission given by Jesus in the last chapter of the book of John.

What are some practical aspects of being poor of spirit? It may mean taking an anger management course, getting grief counseling, finding help to get free of a secret addiction, confiding to a friend about a need, or realising that you haven't the parenting skills you thought you had and seeking help: these are all ways of recognising that you are human, flawed, and in need of support. Being poor of spirit is the antithesis of pride, which hinders any progress. Where poverty of spirit has been replaced by pride, there can be no blessing. It is true in any area of life. Even those who have no faith but realize they need help can, in their brokenness, find some relief somewhere since so many of our society's organisations that offer help are of Christian origin or have some Christian influence.

For some this may need fasting as well. "Poor" here has the connotation of being spiritually helpless. Isaiah 66:1b says, "Where *is* the house that ye build unto me? And where *is* the place of my rest?" Verse 2 says, "but to this *man* will I look, *even* to *him that is* poor and of a contrite spirit, and trembleth at my word." God wants to dwell—to "rest"—within this kind of person. Jesus exemplified poverty of spirit in a somewhat different way since, unlike us, He was sinless. We are told that He who was "in the form of God . . . made himself of no reputation, and took upon him the form of a servant" (Philippians 2:6-7). And "though he was rich, yet for your sakes he became poor, that ye through his poverty might be made rich" (2 Corinthians 8:9). The contrasts are there for us to consider and to meditate on.

In short, the poverty of spirit here indicates a divinely-revealed awareness of our desperate need. The second beatitude illustrates more about our response, which is to be one of repentance for trying to fill our need with other things, and of submission to God and acceptance of His provision through the death and resurrection of Jesus Christ.

This first beatitude points to an important characteristic of the kingdom: the kingdom of God includes healing. Being truly poor in spirit grants access to that healing, and any earthly organisations outside of the influence of the kingdom of God can only give a temporary salve. Ultimately, full repentance brings full blessing. Full faith brings full salvation.

MOURNING

"Blessed are they that mourn: for they shall be comforted."

Objection: *"Mourning means someone or something close to us has died, or we have in some way experienced loss. Though we know that it's part of life, there's no actual merit in it. Why would God, if He exists and if He really loves us, actually want us to experience the devastation of loss? How can a metaphysical idea that you call 'God' give people comfort? What do you mean by 'comfort' anyway?"*

Response: Like poverty of spirit, mourning is a means of connecting us to reality. Normal grief is not meant to be denied, as it is part of normal human feelings. For the believer in Jesus, however, it drives us into the heart of God, who has intense and eternal love. Nothing and no one can comfort us like Him. He calls Himself the "God of all comfort" (2 Corinthians 1:3), and reveals the "comfort of the Holy Ghost" (Acts 9:31) and the "comfort of the scriptures" (Romans 15:4). However, mourning has a meaning here that speaks to how we get near to God. By it we experience His love and prove for ourselves His reality. "Comfort" is the word used for what God gives us when we respond to His call to mourn for what He mourns for. Jesus wept over sin and sickness and death—none of which are God's ultimate plan for humankind; in fact, God works to alleviate them, and makes it clear that all three will eventually be eradicated.

What could Jesus have meant by there being blessing for mourners? He knew this human emotion. He mourned along with the others at the time of His friend Lazarus's death. Yet, knowing that He was going to raise Lazarus, it was not so much the death of Lazarus that moved Him—He was about to deal with that—but it was the sight of Mary and others weeping. Seeing them, "he groaned in the spirit, and was troubled . . . Jesus wept . . . Jesus therefore again groaning within himself cometh to the grave" (John 11:33, 35, 38). He was weeping for them all, just as Paul later wrote, "weep with them that weep" (Romans 12:15).

He was characterised by a compassion that made Him weep over Jerusalem as well, and His whole ministry was one of great sympathy for humanity's suffering. Indeed, the prophet Isaiah described Him as "a man of sorrows, and acquainted with grief" (Isaiah 53:3), and again, that "He hath borne our griefs, and carried our sorrows" (v. 4). He knew what it was like, but His mourning was mixed with a depth of sorrow that only He could know due to His unique ministry. He grieved for you and for me—for our suffering, for our grief, and for our sins—to the point of dying on a cross for us.

"To mourn" in Greek is *pentheo,* which simply means "to grieve or mourn". "Comforted" is *parakaio,* which is made up of *para* "with", and *kaio* "call", i.e., "to be called near" i.e., "invited by hortation (encouragement/exhortation) or consolation".

It would be stretching the context here to say that *anyone* who mourns in this world is automatically a candidate for God's consolation and help. The ungodly, the hardened criminal, the stubborn dictator—all mourn to some degree when they lose someone close to them, but here it can only have ultimate meaning for those who are believers or who are in the process of believing. Further, this beatitude follows along perfectly from the previous one. Mourning also involves more than sadness for sin, which alone is not enough. Contrition is also a type of mourning, which must then lead to full repentance and change—a turning around of one's life, and a continued sense of one's own poverty of spirit and dependence on the God of the universe for salvation. Those who truly mourn, for the right reasons, find themselves being "called near". They find themselves being invited into His presence.

To mourn is to grieve—another word for the same thing. What do we normally grieve over? We grieve the loss of loved ones and friends, loss of aspects of our physical health, loss of innocence, loss of property, lands, or control of our country, loss of national identity, moral decline of our communities, straying children, past sins, and missed opportunities—there is no one in the world exempt from at least some of these, and the very fact of our mourning over any of them is an opportunity for God to comfort. He can do it for anyone, anywhere. The only caveat is that it is not automatic, as already noted. God seemingly stands afar off and *parakaio*—calls us near. When we come to Him as James 4:8 says—"draw nigh to God and He will draw nigh to you"—He draws near to us. The call is to all, believers and unbelievers alike, because He knows that unremitted grief can consume us. Grief for a period is normal, but all grief of whatever intensity must drive us to Him who is "calling us near". Some people can barely function in life due to the grief of losing someone or something, or over their past choices, but excessive or prolonged grief is truly crippling. Additionally, if we do not come near to God, there is a danger not only of grief being prolonged unnecessarily but also of our becoming numb. Numbness means we have become overtaken and have reduced responsiveness to others, including those who need us to be responsive. There is a limit, and God wants us to come to Him for help when we feel that we have reached our limit, or better still, well *before* that point. That is why He draws us near.

"Near" Him, we find comfort, consolation, encouragement, and peace. He has the ability to take the sting away from the experience. Jesus also called the Holy Spirit "the Comforter"—*paraklētos* i.e., intercessor, consoler, advocate, comforter (John 14:16, 26; 15:26; 16:7). This "comforting" is just one of the roles of the Holy Spirit. We saw in the last chapter that the word *pneuma* means "breath/vital principle of life". This is also the word used for the Spirit of God—the *pneuma* or "breath" of God. However, He is described here as a Paraclete, or helper, rendered "Comforter" in some versions. The word "comfort" today might remind us of curling up on a sofa with a hot drink and some chocolates on a cold day, finding a shoulder to lean on or a sympathetic ear, getting soothing advice, or even, for some, the false comfort of drugs or alcohol. What we often think of may be far from the original intended meaning. So, it is very important for us to understand what God is really wanting to do here in "comforting" us, for it is not *only* consolation.

The English word "comfort" has changed over the centuries, and at the time of the King James translation (1611), it still had much of its older and sturdier meaning, which came from the Latin root *fortis*, meaning strong or courageous.[7] Similarly, the Greek word *paraklētos* is from a verb whose main use was for rallying and encouraging soldiers who were about to go into battle.

So, it is much more than *only* finding solace in times of distress or grief, significant though that is. More importantly, it carries the concept of helping us back onto our feet, and keeping us there! Like *parakaio, paraklētos* speaks of exhortation, being strengthened and summoned back into action and service.

Anyone may come, but the ungodly, the hardened criminal, the dictator . . . if they do not come but remain unrepentant, can *never* receive comfort from God. Coming to Him means believing that He exists and that He wants us to come. He says, "Come to me".

The first point of mourning then must be over our own sin and spiritual poverty.

> In that day did the Lord GOD of hosts call to weeping, and to mourning, and to baldness, and to girding with sackcloth: And behold, joy and gladness, slaying oxen, and killing sheep, eating flesh, and drinking wine: let us eat and drink; for tomorrow we shall die. And it was revealed in mine ears by the Lord of hosts, Surely this iniquity shall not be purged from you till ye die, saith the LORD God of hosts (Isaiah 22:12-14).

---

7   This is where we get words such as "fort" and "fortify" from.

"Be afflicted, and mourn, and weep: let your laughter be turned to mourning, and *your* joy to heaviness. Humble yourselves in the sight of the Lord, and he shall lift you up" (James 4:9-10).

This beatitude is stating that those who grieve will be called near to God. And as we respond to that call, we can receive the blessing of God's encouragement and consolation—His hugs of love. None of us can escape the causes; it is how we respond that determines our ongoing condition. This is never an easy issue, but the offer of Jesus is there. God has made provision for assuaging the reality of human loss. In our world, mourning is a daily part of life. Someone somewhere is grieving at this very moment. Sometimes, it is a daily aspect of our personal lives, too.

For this reason, Jesus gave us the Lord's Prayer, which is powerful and effective when prayed deliberately and with the cries and sighs of our hearts over the specific aspects of our lives which need remedy. When He said that we should pray "Thy will be done", He was stating that we should make this statement as one of relinquishment, and "Thy kingdom come" is a statement of hope. These affect our emotions and our intentions as they become purposeful statements of change. "Thy will be done" is also close to a command, and "Thy kingdom come" feels as if it is actually clearing away all spiritual opposition as well as the opposition of our sinfulness—to clear the way for the King to move and do His will!

How else do we mourn? When we read the tragic stories in a newspaper—the terrible misfortunes, accidents, deaths, the tragedy of a fallen world—these are reasons enough. "Jesus wept", and so will we if our heart is after His. It is not for ourselves in this case, but rather to mourn with those who mourn. Consider the afflictions of others more than your own, especially as so many have no understanding of or access to the comfort of God. The provisions are for those who believe. The "kingdom of heaven" and "comfort" both speak of healing, wholeness, triumph, and ultimate joy. This is the *parakaio* of our God.

Blessed *be* God, even the Father of our Lord Jesus Christ, the Father of mercies, and the God of all comfort; Who comforteth us in all our tribulation, that we may be able to comfort them which are in any trouble, by the comfort wherewith we ourselves are comforted of God. (2 Corinthians 1:3-4)

Now our Lord Jesus Christ himself, and God, even our Father, which hath loved us, and hath given *us* everlasting consolation and good hope through grace, Comfort your hearts, and stablish you in every good word and work. (2 Thessalonians 2:16-17)

MEEKNESS

"Blessed are *the meek: for they shall inherit the earth."*

Objection*: "Meekness is weakness! Meek people are wimps. Toughness is what counts. You have to be hard and staunch to survive in this world. Everyone knows that it's the toughest dude on the block who gets the respect. Being one up on the next bloke is how you get ahead. The only alternative is to sink or get crushed. What's wrong with being proud of who you are and what you've done? What value has meekness in this dog-eat-dog world?"*

Response: Meekness is not weakness. It is not about being passive, or lying down and letting everybody walk over you. It's something totally different. In fact, to be truly meek is to have a particular type of strength—a faith and confidence that God Himself is your strength and, if need be, your vindicator. It also speaks of self-control. Jesus was the most powerful man on earth, and yet also the meekest man on earth during His incarnation.

Jesus modeled the next of His beatitudes for all to see; indeed, this one, He is particularly well known for.

He has often been called "meek and mild", although it is doubtful that the "mild" part applies. The word was "lowly", meaning "of low estate" in Zechariah 9:9 and in Matthew 11:29.

But mild?

He was certainly not mild in His dealings with the demon-possessed, or with desperate people needing radical change in their lives, or with the arrogant, downright dangerous Pharisees and "lawyers". Even so, He was without a doubt the meekest man. But what kind of meek? Was it really what we normally think of when we hear the word? Because He also demonstrated incredible power.

Let's study further. This beatitude speaks of a different inheritance than the first. There, it was the kingdom of heaven for the poor in spirit. Here, however, it is the earth that the meek "inherit". God wants His kingdom to come on earth, but the pattern so far in these first three is: first, heaven; third, earth; and in between, suffering (mourning) and comfort.

The word for "meek" is *praos*, meaning "gentle, mild, meek". As it refers to things, it means "gentle" e.g., a gentle breeze or gentle voice. As it refers to people, it means *mild, gracious, kindly. Praotes* is "meekness"—not only "outward behaviour or natural disposition, but an in-wrought grace of the soul, a temper of spirit in which we accept his dealings with us as good, and therefore without disputing or resisting."[8] Also, from the same source: "it is only the humble heart which is also the meek and which, as such, does not fight against God and more or less struggle and contend with him."[9] It is connected with the word *tapeinophrosune* (humility).

Praotes does not denote weakness, but it is the "fruit of power". Jesus could be meek because He "had the infinite resources of God at his command".[10] The words "gentle, mild, meek" in English do not seem to portray the full meaning of *praotes* or *praus*. Rather, "the man who is *praus* is always angry at the right time and never angry at the wrong time."[11] That man is under perfect control. So "behind the gentleness is the strength of steel".[12] Moses was just

8   Vine, 1952, p. 727
9   Vine, p. 728
10   Ibid.
11   Barclay, 1964, p. 241
12   Ibid.

such a man, the "meekest" man upon the earth according to Numbers 12:3, yet he operated with strength and decisiveness when needed. This is not just self-control, but God-control. "It is not spineless gentleness, a sentimental fondness, a passive quietism. It is strength under control."[13] Vine states that this meekness is the opposite of self-assertiveness and self-interest. It could be added that it is also opposite to self-centeredness; it is simply not occupied with self anymore.

This was the meekness that Jesus had, and that He speaks of here.

It's a bit like a great body-building, weight-lifting muscle man being perfectly calm and controlled in normal situations, but using his strength when it is really needed to help someone. Here, there is no need to prove oneself. There's no insecurity, macho bragging or swaggering aggressiveness—in fact quite the opposite, but the strength is there when it is needed.

Praus was used "for a beast which has been tamed"[14]. It is similar to a horse that has been broken in. The animal was wild and strong to begin with, and then it was broken in. It is still strong, but now yields for a greater purpose and use to its master. Our souls are also untamed before our encounter with Jesus. We are Jacob before we become Israel—supplanters and tricksters before we become princes with God. Yet meekness is certainly not fawning obsequiousness and lily-livered acquiescence. It is listed as a fruit of the Spirit in Galatians 5:22-23, alongside "gentleness" (which means "kind, good of heart, easy, gracious"). Meekness is from the Spirit of God, not from ourselves. It is not the same as being "poor in spirit", though that is the starting place and the daily reference point to retain the kingdom of God in our hearts. Mourning is the means of attaining this poverty of spirit and is part of the "breaking in" process. Meekness is the result.

The followers of Jesus have many of God's resources available to them, but God's power within requires meekness on their part. If they allow themselves

---

13   Ibid, p. 242
14   Barclay, Ibid.

to be proud then they risk losing those resources. Pride and God do not mix, but pride, self, and Satan do. Again, this meekness is not grovelling, just as poverty of spirit is not having an emotional breakdown, and mourning is not misery or a permanent state of despair or bitterness. Reviewing the Greek meanings of these words helps us to get the real gist of them. What do they really say about our character and how we approach the Creator God? Are these qualities real and active within us? The resources from "the kingdom of heaven" are for the poor in spirit, nearness to the Creator is for mourners, and a great promise is there for the meek.

Psalm 37:11 and 22 contain exactly the same statement as this beatitude. In fact, it is seen in various forms six times—in verses 3, 9, 11, 22, 29, and 34, and hinted at in verse 27. The word for "earth" in the Greek is *gē* (*eretz* in Hebrew), meaning simply "earth, country, ground, land, or world".[15] Adam was from the "earth" i.e., *ge* – the arable land, the soil (1 Corinthians 15:47). Interestingly, the word "humility" is from "humus" (Lat.) i.e., ground, earth, soil.

Therefore, meekness is akin to humility, and the reward for meekness is the land from whence we came. The implication is of blessing in our earthly existence, and this was certainly the case for the righteous person in the Old Testament. Yet, here we have it again in the first speech of our Lord when He was on earth. The words can be taken literally—the earth itself belongs to the meek. Even now, in our present earthly existence, this can mean favour from God, a home filled with good things. It can also speak of abundant provision, an inheritance to pass down to your children's children, and a sense that "all things are yours" (1 Corinthians 3:21). This revelation of inheritance is not just to take, but also to receive because "ye are Christ's" (1 Corinthians 3:23) and your body and spirit "belong to God" (1 Corinthians 6:20). We belong to Christ, from whom are all good things.

Who inherited land in the Bible? Abraham, Joseph, the children of Israel, Aaron, and Joshua. As the children of Abraham, we may receive the same,

---

15   We get the words "geology, geography, and geometry" from this word *ge*.

though we may not know how it will happen. It is not a case of evicting people from some physical land and taking over, but rather inheriting all that God has for us as individuals. Are the "meek" here plural or are they individuals? Is the "land" physical or spiritual? God deals with families and nations as well, so perhaps there is something here for them too—if a nation is willing to be meek, if a family is willing to be in the right place of meekness before God. "Meekness promotes wealth, comfort, and safety, even in this world."[16]

In Mark 10:29 and 30 we are told that those who have given up everything to follow Jesus "shall receive a hundredfold now in this time . . . lands, with persecutions; and in the world to come eternal life." Here, Jesus makes it clear the "inheritance" is *now in this time*, as contrasted with "the world to come". This double blessing for leaving lands, house, brethren, etc. "for my sake, and the gospel's" involves the act of turning around and going in a different direction. For some, this is physical; for the sake of the gospel, someone may have to *physically* leave their house, and their father and mother. Someone who has been rejected by their immediate family because of their faith may have to do this too. However, since Jesus includes wife and children in this statement, it cannot possibly mean an outright or even subtle rejection of them, as we are commanded to love and care for our families (it also omits the word "husband"!). It is the *spiritual* intent of the passage that should be considered, and what is figuratively implied is a new and greater focus superseding earthly loyalties. The love for Jesus and the gospel is that much stronger than all else. So, it follows that the fulfilment of this verse, of "a hundredfold now in this time", has manifestations both figurative and literal, but though there is blessing now and blessing to come, there is no guarantee that the initial blessing will be all plain sailing, for He adds "with persecutions".

The word for "inherit" is *klēronomēo,* which means "to receive by lot, to receive as one's own". The ones who are meek in the *praus* sense are the ones who have dominion and subdue the earth, which was the original mandate

---

16   Matthew Henry, 1710

for us as human beings. There is no place where they will go where the Spirit of God will not be there with them. They will evict the spiritual foes (Satan and demons) from their homes and properties as well as from their businesses and spheres of influence. In this way, they will inherit the earth. They will completely own the ground they walk on as they do justly, love mercy, and walk humbly with their God (Micah 6:8). Satan is their foe, but he doesn't win over them. *They* are in charge. *They* are royalty, and they walk, talk, act, and think like royalty. There is nothing that will defeat them because God is not the author of defeat, but of strength, power, and authority. Here is the inheritance of the saints. Though this life is not permanent, one day they will also rule with the King of kings: *"And the kingdom and dominion, and the greatness of the kingdom under the whole heaven, shall be given to the people of the saints of the most high,* whose kingdom *is* an everlasting kingdom, and all dominions [rulers] shall serve and obey him."* (Daniel 7:27, author's emphasis. See also Daniel 7:22).

"Inherit the earth" could also mean that abundant provision in normal circumstances is the believer's privilege. The world sees the meek as weak, but the irony is that at present, it is the proud who mostly seek to dominate the earth through fear and other means. Yet they are the ones who, in God's economy, eventually suffer loss.

If we were to take Jesus's words literally, it would be the meek who end up getting the lot, not by their own effort or virtue, but by the quality of their character, their attitude, simply their be-attitude. If it is to have a literal future, then how it will happen is yet to be seen. Inheriting the land speaks of stability and permanence. It brings up images of individuals, families, and communities having land, holding land, developing land, making the land prosper and themselves prospering because of the land. It speaks of people blessing the land by being able stewards of it, and of the land in turn blessing them by its God-intended purpose of production and abundance. It speaks of houses and gardens, fields, flowers, families, children, grandchildren, livestock, pets, and beauty everywhere. These are the pictures that "inherit the land" suggests.

It suggests peace and stability. It is the opposite of being landless, of being a refugee, rejected, a nomad, abjectly poor, homeless, and hungry. It is also the opposite of arrogant, super-rich landowners oppressing the poor, because although they may flourish in this life, their heritage is not one of the joy of God in their or their descendants' lives. The meek who inherit the earth have the humility of Jesus in their hearts, and their eventual inheritance is eternal.

So where do we start now on this earth?

"The Lord upholdeth all that fall, and raiseth up all *those that be* bowed down" (Psalm 145:14) and "He will regard the prayer of the destitute, and not despise their prayer" (Psalm 102:17).

This is the start.

Psalm 51 states that God will not despise a broken heart. This is cast as an understatement, for why indeed would a loving God actually *despise* a broken heart? Instead, He "heals the broken-hearted", and Jesus said that He came for that very purpose, and "to set at liberty them that are bruised" (Luke 4:18). But this message is *only* to the meek: "good tidings unto the meek" (Isaiah 61:1). For them, there is also the "oil of joy" instead of "mourning", and "a garment of praise" instead of "the spirit of heaviness" (v. 3). Then "they shall build the old wastes, raise up the former desolations . . . repair the waste cities, the desolations of many generations" (v. 4).

So, God makes mourners into builders—*re*builders and repairers. He is rebuilding, raising up, and repairing, *in* us first and then *through* us. Out of sadness and failure, you can find something which needs fixing or someone who needs help. Many places and people in the world are desolate and wasted, needing someone who's "been through it" to help them get up again and start anew. Thus you take beauty, the oil of joy, and the garment of praise into those situations, and you become "trees of righteousness". God is ultimately glorified and "*men* . . . call you the Ministers of our God" (v. 6).

SUMMARY OF THE FIRST THREE BEATITUDES

In review of these first three beatitudes, it is clear that Jesus has started His first "professional development" session with His disciples on the most serious note and with absolutely the most crucial issues of life in mind: our approach to God; our relation to the kingdom of heaven; our relation to the challenges and disappointments and losses that life brings; our reaction to the problem of sin within ourselves and within others; and our relation to others through "controlled strength". An unbelieving, proud person will mourn and grieve like any others but will not be "called near" to receive the comfort of God because they have not yet entered into a covenant with Him by first making themselves "poor in spirit", i.e., "beggars for the vital principle of life" that is in Christ. They have no hope of "inheriting the earth", whatever that may imply, because they have not had divine meekness imparted to them. Rather, they will ultimately have loss.[17]

---

17   And this is true of over-proud nations as well, though for a time they may prosper (or appear to), or rule over others, there comes a time when they are brought low (see, for example, Ezekiel 32).

RIGHTEOUSNESS

"Blessed are *they which do hunger and thirst after righteousness:*
for they shall be filled".

Objection: *"Righteousness? What's that? What you mean is being holier-than-thou! All those goody-goody Christians going around telling everyone else what to do or trying to 'convert the heathen'! Who are they to tell anyone anything? They're all just a bunch of self-righteous, religious hypocrites. Get real; everyone tells a few lies now and then! And everyone has a few secret sins! That's just life. Who's to say what's right and wrong anyway?"*

Response: Imagine that you had committed offenses, yet ones that the law of the land didn't worry about, but God did. Those grubby habits that no one knew about except you, and horrible little thoughts that plagued your life and sometimes even surprised you yourself, along with words that came out of your mouth that you wished never would because they embarrassed you and embarrassed or hurt others. Imagine now that God looks lovingly on you as a great judge and asks you, "Are you really sorry about these things in your life?" You answer, "yes". Then He says in a tender voice, "Not guilty! Forgiven of all sins. Jesus has paid your penalty for you and gives you the power to break sinful habits!" How would you feel? If you were hungry for forgiveness and freedom from sin, and God gave it to you, along with the ability to not live a life of sin anymore and to be at peace with Him, with others, and with yourself, then you would have this righteousness that Jesus spoke of.

So far in the Beatitudes, Jesus has reiterated some easily remembered statements that were also mentioned in the Scriptures of the Old Testament. Now, He speaks of a state of constant, daily hunger and thirst after righteousness (*dikaiosunē*).

Originally spelt "rightwiseness", righteousness means whatever is right and just. The word for righteousness is the same throughout the New Testament, and the word "just" is the same in meaning. "Justified" is *dikaioo*, meaning "to render innocent". The Old Testament meaning of righteous is in the sense of moral virtue, and in the Greek, it means "desiring to be innocent, holy, justified, and equitable in character."

So we should hunger and thirst for:

- Innocence
- Remittance or release of sins
- Holiness
- Right standing with God

Is righteousness possible outside of the cross? No, not in the sense of its complete fulfilment of the law and of God's requirements, because no man or woman could ever keep *all* the law *all* of the time in either its requirements for daily living or in its implications for the holiness of the inner person. Only a work of God—the death and resurrection of Jesus—could provide atonement for sin and release us from our guilt and shame for failing to keep God's law. Then, standing on the other side of the cross, free, pardoned and justified, we could accept the declaration of "righteous".[18]

The faith imparted to us by God Himself enabled us to receive the fullness of His salvation through no merit of our own—though not without our

---

18   The Old Testament Passover prefigured the cross and was a provision for all who had faith in the blood of the sacrificed lamb.

responsiveness to His call, our acceptance of it, obviously. Then, after being *declared* righteous through God's forgiveness, we can go on to *live* righteous lives and bring forth works of righteousness, *fulfilling* the law in our hearts, just as Jesus came to fulfil the law; so, when He lives in us, He fulfills the law by His Spirit in us.

However, there are inevitably still areas of unresponsiveness in us where we still have not the full integrity required by the law. These areas are only brought to light by the Spirit and by our *knowing* and *understanding* the moral law of the Old Testament. Then, we know where we are wrong, and we allow His Spirit to transform and build our character so that those weak spots are filled. This "filling" came with the arrival of the Holy Spirit *after* Jesus's death and resurrection. Before that, it appears that followers of Jesus could only be filled with a "measure" of it. The hungering and thirsting was only filled in reality after Jesus's crucifixion. Now, we can be filled to the full. God has many things to fill us up with, but the first is righteousness. The word is translated "alms" in Matthew 6:1 and, in its practical outworking, is there portrayed in the way we approach giving, prayer, and fasting.

Righteousness is imparted to us after our repentance, and our standing with God then becomes "right"—clean and clear in His sight. The cross is behind us and heaven in front of us. Again, many try to be righteous, to be filled with the Spirit, to help others, and to be pure, but they haven't taken steps one, two, and three first, i.e., "poverty of spirit", "mourning' and "meekness".

Jesus was, in this beatitude, drawing again on Old Testament imagery, but it was to have a future fulfilment as a result of His life, His words, and His death and resurrection. Psalm 37:25 says, "I have been young, and *now* am old; yet have I not seen the righteous forsaken", and verse 29, "The righteous shall inherit the land." Righteousness and meekness are linked. "The meek will he guide in judgment: and the meek will he teach his way" (Psalm 25:9), and "all the paths of the Lord *are* mercy and truth unto such as keep his covenant and his testimonies" (v. 10).

When people go off onto doctrinal tangents, join cults, or accept offshoot alternatives, they almost always miss the first part of Jesus's teachings in the Sermon on the Mount. Skipping over the section on brokenness (poverty of spirit, mourning, meekness), they try to go straight into righteousness or good works. Without the brokenness, they carry pride and become an offence and a shame to the gospel. The first three beatitudes point to the cross. They looked forward to the cross at the time, as did all of God's requirements for those who had faith. True mourning, for example, takes place when we look at what Jesus did for us. We cannot skip over the cross and think that we will be on the right side of God. The cross comes first. Then, with sin and self all dealt with there, the slate is swept clean and that's the time, if our heart is right, when we start hungering and thirsting for God.

Although the Beatitudes are not necessarily a series of steps, it is possible that they are in the order they are for a reason. Those who heard them were from a culture that knew about these things. No commandment is given, only promises based on what people *are,* but no one is born like that. No one is born pure; there is choice involved. Righteousness is about being right with Him. The righteousness of God is who He is—faithful, true, and holy. It comes close also to "justice and judgment". God requires righteousness of us (Matthew 6:33), and faith is the vehicle that carries us into that place. Of course, what we do also counts; Jesus put some on His right because of what they *did*: they showed mercy, fed the hungry, gave drink to the thirsty, clothed the poor, visited the sick and the prisoners (Matthew 25:31-46). The others He put on His left. Though someone may be justified by faith, that faith is still pronounced "dead" if there are no corresponding "works" (James 2:17, 26).

Our mourning has been replaced by the garment of praise, and we are being "called" i.e., declared, "trees of righteousness". We do not achieve righteousness—we are declared so as a result of Jesus's atonement, as clearly stated by Paul later in the New Testament. The words he uses are "justified" and "imputed", as in Romans 3:24 and 4:24 (see also 2 Corinthians 5:21). The state of righteousness is not just to be desired, but in fact hungered and thirsted after.

God is there waiting to satisfy both our hunger and our thirst, but He doesn't tell us here *what* those who are in this situation will be "filled" with, only that they will be "filled", but we could safely assume that, in the first instance, it is to be filled with that very thing we are hungering and thirsting after—rightness with God. Also, "He will fulfil the desire of them that fear him" (Psalm 145:19), and in Psalm 107:9 "he satisfieth the longing soul, and filleth the hungry soul with goodness." The Hebrew word for "filled" is *chortaze* and it speaks of "satisfaction and completeness", specifically of food, so here it is metaphorical. Our word "plenty" has the same derivation.

Spiritual hunger has similarities with physical hunger. It can be just as intense and if not satisfied, can be spiritually fatal. The "food" must be good and wholesome, just like our physical food. Some say that righteousness is the same as social justice (i.e., Matthew 25:31-46 but without the justifying faith). However, we cannot be "filled" with social justice. If you strongly desire and have an appetite for right standing with God, then you will be filled with the rightness and holiness of heart that comes from right standing with Him.

In summary, God's people were called "righteous" in the Old Testament often by what they did (e.g., Psalm 106:31), so although they also were justified by their faith, they still actually had to *work* righteousness. The latter is similar today, but, as described above, the righteousness is initially granted to us by what Jesus did on the cross. However, it is no use saying, "I am the righteousness of God in Christ Jesus", and then doing some unrighteous act! This is vanity, and in that case, your right standing with God on the basis of Jesus's blood is invalidated by your wrongdoing. Rather, *because* we have the righteousness given to us on condition of our repentance and faith in the blood of Jesus, we then *do* righteous things and *live* righteously as a matter of course.

None of this would be possible without the overarching gift of God's grace. Grace (*charis*) brings the unearned favour of the Creator to us, His creation.

Mercy is the action of alleviating the power of sin and its consequences. Grace is how God is able to "call us near" to Himself without us ever having *earned* the privilege. This is because He is good and He loves us freely. However, it is a "tough love" which cannot be taken advantage of or taken presumptively. Everything from our calling, to our repentance, to the faith imparted to us is the result of grace (Galatians 1:15; 2 Timothy 1:9; 2:25; Ephesians 2:8-9).[19] By this grace alone we can live a righteous life that is pleasing to Him. A prime example of grace in the Scripture is that of Abraham and his wife, Sarah. God changed their names from Abram (meaning *exalted father*) to Abraham, (meaning *father of many nations*), and his wife's name from Sarai (meaning *dominative*) to Sarah (meaning *princess/queen/nobility*). In each case the difference was the added "h", the breath of God, the *hei* (ה), the letter of grace (see page 14). It was this new impetus from God in their lives which transformed their experience and their destiny, and it will do the same for any of us, no matter who we are.

So, what causes us to hunger and thirst for this? Firstly, in the beginning we know we *need* it and we don't *have* it. Secondly, we contend with a sinful nature, and God's Spirit within us contends for mastery on a daily basis. This creates a desire for righteousness.

The simple truth is it only happens if we desire it. If you don't desire better health, you'll never have it. If you don't desire a good job, you'll never have it, at least it is highly unlikely (though not impossible) that it will simply fall into your lap. We have to first be like a starving person or someone nearly fainting with thirst; we must be desperate. Then, God can fill us. It then becomes just like our regular daily hunger that makes us eat our physical food, and the more we work or exercise, the healthier our appetite will be. We know our need. Our hunger and thirst returns, and we are filled again daily from the table God has prepared for us, as Psalm 23:1,3,5 and Psalm 63:1 state.

---

19   Douglas, 1962

THE FIFTH

MERCY

"Blessed are *the merciful: for they shall obtain mercy."*

Objection: *"To be merciful is fine in certain circumstances, but it all depends on the situation. Like when you want to save some whales or endangered species, or help some poor people or the disabled and elderly. Then, it's fine. It depends on what you mean by "mercy" though. I mean, euthanasia can be merciful, and it fits in with the facts of evolution that we all live by—or at least most of us! But sometimes you just have to be ruthless, especially in business, or with people who cross you. And there's not much room for mercy when you're competing with others in sports or in the marketplace, and none in times of political or regional conflict."*

Response: From the human perspective, being merciful is ultimately about showing empathy, which is when we understand the feelings of others. It makes you a better person, more astute, kinder, and altogether better to be around. Others will respect you and show you favour and trust because you deal mercifully. Being ruthless makes you hard, and hardness makes you unlikeable, and you end up receiving the same thing you give. Conversely, if you give mercy, you will receive it too. However, this mercy is not only about being sympathetic and having pity on others, but also having a real desire to alleviate their suffering. This is what God's mercy is. In fact, the mercy spoken about here goes much further than mere human kindness, though it includes that. There is a deeper element to it.

So, we come to the fifth beatitude, and there are some key verses which link in with this. Mercy is the result of true righteousness. It is dynamic compassion and grace. *Eleēmōn* (merciful) means "not simply possessed of pity, but actively compassionate".[20] In Luke 6:36, "merciful" is given a stronger term in Greek: *oktirmōn*.[21] "Mercy" (as in "receive mercy") is the noun *eleos*: "the outward manifestation of pity; it assumes need on the part of him who receives it, and resources adequate to meet the need on the part of him who shows it".[22] So, mercy cannot be given unless there are resources available to, or from, the giver to *be* given.

Having established exactly what it is, we find that it is all through the Bible and is mentioned in reference to both God and to human relations. Psalm 136 uses it twenty-six times in a row: "for His mercy endureth forever". The reality is that in this world, some people and some nations lack this quality, yet Jesus said that the nations themselves would be judged by how much or how little they show it. Yes, feeding the hungry, clothing the naked, and visiting the sick and the prisoner are acts of righteousness, but even more so are they acts of mercy. It is not enough to show mercy to your own kin, but not to others.

Everything Jesus did was ultimately out of mercy, although it is not so easy to see it in the way He dealt with the Pharisees. One incident often used to show a distinction between the Old Covenant and the New is that of Jesus's treatment of the woman found in adultery in John chapter 8. Here, Jesus showed mercy to the woman who, it would appear, was truly broken in spirit ("poor in spirit"), but He did not appear to show mercy to

---

20 Vine, 734
21 There is also the adjective *hileos*, meaning "cheerful, propitious, gracious" e.g., Hebrews 8:12, and one instance of the verb *hilaakomai,* meaning "to conciliate, atone, be propitious", e.g., Luke 18:13.
22 Vine, 732

her accusers—the scribes and Pharisees. They slunk away at His rebuke, knowing full well that they also had sin in their hearts. They were not "qualified" to be the executioners, or even to throw one stone. Here, Jesus was not saying that the law of Moses was wrong when it prescribed stoning for certain offenses, which is what it did. The implication, however, was clearly that there would come a day—indeed, it had already come in a sense by His presence—when, firstly, religious leaders would no longer be the ones doing the condemning, let alone dishing out the punishment, as that would become the decision of various future governments as they shaped their laws based on what they considered to be right or wrong. Secondly, future laws would begin to have a distinct element of mercy in them that was not so characteristic of the Mosaic system of laws where people's transgressions were made to be seen (rightly) as particularly serious in contrast to the holiness of God. This was exemplary, but there had been an inherent severity there as well, and the old system of animal sacrifices was imperfect.

The perfection came with Jesus Christ. The perfection came with mercy.

It is also significant that as the self-righteous rulers in the temple waited for Jesus's answer regarding their question about the law of Moses, He "stooped down, and with *his* finger wrote on the ground" instead of answering them.[23] We do not know what it was that Jesus wrote, but His action was highly symbolic. Here was someone not only the equal of Moses, but far more, who like God, wrote with His finger.[24] It could have been the finer points of the law that He wrote, or aspects of mercy that were already there in the Torah, perhaps even these beatitudes, or a disclosure of the personal sins that had been lurking in the hearts of the scribes and Pharisees. Whatever it was, it was a studied pause that gave dramatic effect to His subsequent stinging words that echo down through time to all religious leaders everywhere: "He

---

23   The law of Moses was also written "with the finger of God" in Exodus 31:18 .
24   See Hebrews 3:3

that is without sin among you, let him first cast a stone at her." The woman was then free to "go, and sin no more".[25]

While mercy is given freely by God, those who constantly rebel against it can eventually find themselves on the other side of it, voluntarily removing themselves from its touch. We can be merciful when we have experienced the kingdom of heaven, God's comfort, the grace of God in giving us many blessings, and the righteousness of God. If we are still not merciful after claiming that we have received all this, then somewhere we have missed it. Our contrition has not been real contrition, mourning and meekness not real mourning and meekness, and our hunger and thirst not true hunger and thirst. Somewhere, pride has entered and made us think we have done these things when we have not. Perhaps we repented for selfish reasons, or mourned for our own personal and selfish losses alone and not over our sins and the souls of others.

Proverbs gives us more insight on mercy: "He that hath mercy on the poor, happy *is* he" and "mercy and truth *shall be* to them that devise good" (Proverbs 14:21-22). Proverbs 21:21 states, "He that followeth after righteousness and mercy findeth life, righteousness, and honour." Lastly, Proverbs 28:13 adds, "He that covereth his sins shall not prosper: but whoso confesseth and forsaketh *them* shall have mercy."

God is rich in mercy (Ephesians 2:4). Four times in Scripture we read the blessing "Grace, mercy, *and* peace from God our Father and the Lord Jesus Christ."[26] God's wisdom (the "wisdom from above") is full of mercy (James 3:17), and this mercy comes from "the throne of grace" (Hebrews 4:16).[27] We understand what mercy is in the English language, but there is a divine mercy that is eternal and also reflects the father-heart of God. Because He is merciful to us as His children, so we should be merciful to our own children. Employers should be merciful to their employees, and political leaders to

---

25   The action and words of Jesus also served to affirm her right as a woman to be treated with respect.

26   1 Timothy 1:2; 2 Timothy 1:2; Titus 1:4; 2 John 3

27   The old tabernacle of Israel had a "mercy seat" near where God dwelt (i.e., was especially manifest).

their subjects, but it is not only top down. We should all be merciful to others. A sick parent needs their children's mercy, and we should be merciful to our neighbours, whoever they are. However, we are not told that this is always going to be any easy thing to do!

Mercy implies pity, but it does not mean that if someone does something *un*merciful that they should be smothered with pity; instead, it means quite the opposite! The unmerciful will receive judgement from God. You cannot think that because you do something that negatively impacts others that you will get mercy from God. Some things are set in stone. Although there are some unnecessary and foolish laws in our countries, we have no choice but to follow them unless they contradict our faith, and there are consequences for not obeying them. However, the police will not chase you if you steal your classmate's pencil or if you peek at some pornography, but *you* know that *you* have broken God's laws by doing so. As we have all sinned by breaking God's laws—by our actions and our thoughts, by doing what we should not have and not doing what we should have—we have all received the penalty of "death". It applies to all, because our sins are an offense against God and "the wages of sin *is* death" (Romans 6:23).

We sin because we have a sin nature, but God cannot wink at even one of our smallest sins. He has to exact the penalty, just like the government has to give you a speeding ticket if you have driven too fast. As we have seen, God paid the full penalty for us by dying Himself as a man—Jesus—to pay for our sins.

Here is God's mercy—in the mystery of the cross.

Though He has given a solution, we cannot then say, "Well, He paid for it so I will sin again", because then we crucify Him again in our hearts. His mercy is great as even our next thought of sin will be forgiven, but *only* if we repent, confess it (to Him), and seek to renounce it.

Some of our government laws allow for those who commit a crime to be given early release or privileges for good behaviour, which is a way of showing a type of grace or mercy. Some laws allow leniency for those who plead to be insane and are proven to not be of sound mind. This would appear to be merciful. However, all crime is insanity. No one commits a crime as a result of sane decisions, and all sin is falling short of what God intended us to be.

Mercy is found in forgiveness, in being given a chance for redemption and restoration. However, God's love and mercy are not seen in His taking our sins lightly, because He cannot do that, but in the whole rescue mission that we call "salvation". It is in providing release, restoration, and power for us to have renewed resolve to love Him with all our heart and soul and strength and mind. It includes the ability to *not* habitually commit sin. It is a remedy, not a compromise. "By mercy and truth iniquity is purged" (Proverbs 16:6).

Another key verse to consider here is Micah 6:8, "He hath shewed thee, O man, what *is* good and what doth the LORD require of thee, but to do justly, and to love mercy, and to walk humbly with thy God [or, to humble thyself to walk with God]". In Hosea 4:1-2, God says that He has a "controversy with the inhabitants of the land, because *there is* no truth, nor mercy, nor knowledge of God in the land" but rather "swearing, and lying, and killing, and stealing, and committing adultery". Here, mercy is allied with truth and the knowledge of God, so it is not a sentimental, emotional thing, but rather a solid, spiritual quality that does not exist or operate alone. Again, it is stated in Hosea 6:6, "For I desired mercy, and not sacrifice; and the knowledge of God more than burnt-offerings."

"Sow to yourselves in righteousness, reap in mercy; break up your fallow ground, for *it is* time to seek the LORD till He come and reign righteousness upon you" (Hosea 10:12). Breaking up your "fallow ground" brings us back to being poor in spirit and mourning for all the right reasons. Zephaniah 2:3 says, "Seek ye the LORD, all ye meek of the earth, which have wrought his judgment [otherwise rendered "justice"]; seek righteousness, seek meekness."

God says that He is merciful: "I *am* merciful, saith the LORD" (Jeremiah 3:12). "Your Father . . . is merciful" (Luke 6:36). We are to be merciful as He is merciful.

Proverbs 14:31 says that "He that oppresseth the poor reproacheth his Maker: but he that honoureth him hath mercy on the poor." The prophet Daniel, in the Old Testament, interpreted one of the Babylonian king Nebuchadnezzar's dreams and warned him to "break off thy sins by righteousness, and thine iniquities by shewing mercy to the poor" (Daniel 4:27). The words of a prophetic predecessor of Jesus to a foreign king, the king of Babylon, were the same as the Master's—you must have righteousness *and* mercy.

THE SIXTH

PURITY OF HEART

"Blessed are *the pure in heart: for they shall see God."*

Objection: *"What do you mean by 'purity'? Do you mean we should all become nuns or monks? And as for being single-minded, the Bible just makes you narrow-minded!"*

Response: Purity is about your mental state and your motives, and when you get these right, you can have a very clear picture of who God is and how He works. Assuming God is real, loving, and powerful, who wouldn't want that?

Jesus was the pure and holy Son of God. He was also single-minded in His purpose. The word for "pure" is *katharos,* meaning "pure, cleansed". We get the words "catharsis" and "cathartic" from it. According to William Barclay, this word has a number of meanings in classical Greek:[28]

- Physically clean
- Free from any mixture, e.g., clean water
- Free from debt
- Free from all guilt and pollution
- Ceremonially clean
- Pure in blood, i.e., racially pure

---

28   1964, pp. 170-172. Barclay points out that the word in this beatitude is rendered in the plural, i.e., *katharoi.*

In the New Testament, it is used to communicate:
- Physical cleanliness, e.g., the linen sheet they wrapped Jesus in
- People fit for God's worship and service
- Things fit for Christians to use
- Being innocent of any crime
- Pureness and cleanness of heart and conscience
- Worship offered to God

The Beatitudes are unique because each statement stands on its own, yet we are also seeing how all nine form an integral whole. By interpreting the word "pure" in the light of oft-associated words in other parts of the New Testament, along the lines of real, genuine, unmixed, unadulterated, and unalloyed, Barclay came up with the following summation: "Blessed are those whose motives are absolutely unmixed, whose minds are utterly sincere, who are completely and totally single-minded." In his estimate, this is the most demanding beatitude. Indeed, it goes to the heart of the matter: our motive. Yet this is how we "see" God.

Again, it cannot be of our own doing. According to Job, "the stars are not pure in his sight. How much less man" (25:5-6), and Proverbs 20:9 asks, "Who can say, I have made my heart clean, I am pure from my sin?" This is a rhetorical question; obviously, the answer is "no one." But 2 Samuel 22:27, repeated in Psalm 18:26, tells us that "with the pure thou wilt shew thyself pure".

The word *katharos* is used four times in Revelation, and the Bible encourages us in Philippians 4:8 to think about things which are "pure", although here a different word is used—*hagnos*, meaning clean, with the idea of being innocent, modest, and chaste. The wisdom "from above" is also "pure" (*hagnos*), so we are to keep ourselves in this state. (1 John 3:3; James 3:17; 1 Timothy 5:22). How we arrive at it is the result of our faith in the blood of Jesus, and our immersion in "pure and undefiled" religion, which is defined as "[to visit] the fatherless and the widows" and to keep yourself "unspotted from the world" (James 1:27).

This must be contextualised accordingly. I also believe that the purity Jesus speaks of here is connected to His next discourse about sexual matters (adultery and how we use our eyes). However, all impurity of thought or action (deviation and compromise) in the area of physical intimacy is a result of a lack of singular focus, of being mentally and emotionally swayed this way and that *away* from the original divine intention.

Regarding the reward of this beatitude, to "see God", there are a number of Greek words for "see", but this one is *optimai,* "to gaze" with wide open eyes, as at something remarkable. From this word, we get "optic", "optometry", and "optometrist".[29] It is different from casual vision. In fact, we read in Exodus 33:20 that "there shall no man see me [God], and live", showing that natural man cannot go face to face with God without an intermediary. Of course, we have this in Jesus who is the "mediator between God and men" (1 Timothy 2:5), but here He is saying something new. Here, "see" implies *open access to God,* the *perception and discernment of God,* and the *understanding and personal experience of God.* It is difficult to see from a scriptural perspective how anyone can be pure in heart according to the meaning given here, or in the sense of being clean in mind, heart, and purpose, without them first having gone through a time of brokenness, contrition, humility, and meekness, hungering and thirsting for and receiving the infilling of righteousness, as well as developing a sense of mercy in their relations with others.

How then can a human be pure? By a work of God's grace alone. One does not arrive at a permanent place of purity any more than one remains in a permanent state of brokenness, but it can become a persistent, habitual experience, and more so as we go through a beatitude-filled life. So, the fact that sometimes you have a period of fulfilment and then fail doesn't mean you should give up. Like any other habit of life, it should be pursued and practised daily until it becomes a lifestyle.

---

29   *Strong, 1990*

Having purity of heart is not only having a clean heart, mind, and spirit, but also being undistracted. You have to really want to "see God" to maintain this undistracted mind. In 2 Timothy 1:7, we read that God gives to those who follow Him power, love, and a sound mind, which in Greek is *sōphronismos*, meaning literally "a safe mind", implying a divinely-given self-control — literally, a "saved mind".

To round off these middle three beatitudes, it is clear that righteousness must result in mercy, not self-righteous legalism that leads to people disliking or hating others and ultimately showing little or no mercy. Righteousness must also lead to true purity in both its sense of moral purity as well as godly singlemindedness. All of these, as well as the other beatitudes, are expounded on in the pages that follow them in Matthew chapters 5, 6, and 7. These eight blessings, nine including the additional personalised one on persecution, and the *makarios* (blessedness) centered on the kingdom of heaven, form a succinct introduction to the whole Sermon on the Mount, at the conclusion of which there is a parable of the two house foundations, Jesus being the "rock" foundation. Those who respond with a heart willing to be like Him, who fulfilled all of them, will lay foundations for a godly life. Thus the Beatitudes express Jesus's nature.

There is no reference to the Ten Commandments in the Beatitudes, yet they are mentioned throughout Jesus's discourses. He who is righteous, merciful, and pure will not steal, murder, or defraud, much less adhere himself to a false god. Jesus's disciples knew about these things as they were brought up in Israel, but these words *refine* the commandments, going to the heart of the matter. It is not enough just to have no other gods than Jehovah—one must have *poverty of spirit and meekness*. It is not enough to just not commit murder—one must go completely the opposite direction and *be merciful* to others and not hate or curse, to in fact *love* your neighbour as yourself. It is not enough just to not commit adultery—one must have a *pure heart* where even the look of lust does not occur. It is about the expression of life in honour of the whole law. In fact, where something was *forbidden* in the law, its *opposite was implied*, even commanded. Whatever was *commanded*, its *opposite was forbidden*. For example, honour the Sabbath; therefore, do not work on that day. Nothing is new here for those who knew the law and the prophets, for they had been speaking of mercy, righteousness, and justice for centuries, but no one had ever put it together in the way Jesus was doing here, and no one had ever had a ministry and life with such an abundance of miracles and such a unique claim as Jesus had.

PEACEMAKING

"Blessed are *the peacemakers: for they shall be called the children of God".*

Objection: *"Your 'peacemakers' are mostly do-gooders trying to sort out everyone else's problems when they should be minding their own business and cleaning out their own backyards. People with real, serious issues just need professional counselors, and as for nations with serious disputes, they need multi-national organisations to step in and advise them. So, we already have peacemakers if that's what you mean. Religious people should stay out of it and workers with such organisations shouldn't have any religious bias. What do you mean by 'peacemaker' anyway?"*

Response: Firstly, a true peacemaker helps people to make their peace with their Creator. That should be the goal of every believer: to get people rightly related on the vertical level. On the horizontal, it is a great privilege to have the chance to help mediate between two or more conflicting parties and to bring peace. Whether between members of an organisation, a business, a church, a family, colleagues, siblings, a community, or even warring factions within a nation, you may be thrust into the conflict unwillingly at first, but it could well be God behind it because He knows that you are the person for the job. You can do it well or badly, depending on how you partner with Him and draw on His wisdom. Not only will you gain a sense of personal satisfaction from seeing people and communities reconciled, but it could also mean that people are saved from being casualties or victims, and that a whole cycle of hatred is broken or avoided because of how you personally responded. Sometimes it may depend on you alone, and sometimes you may be put to work with other peacemakers. It may happen only once in your lifetime, or it may become a life calling. You may not get the thanks and accolades that many hope for, but you may also find that there's a satisfaction in anonymity. People may forget you, but you could discover a surprising peace and rest in your own soul. Also, you will experience a real fulfilment in your heart as well as carry an easy conscience as you "love your neighbour" in this way.

While mercy, humility, and justice are to be our practise in life, they also point to qualities of character. There is this to be added: the quality and the *actions* of a peacemaker. Jesus was a peacemaker, but He was also a source of conflict and division amongst those who opposed His teachings. So, what does this mean for us? How should those who follow Him be peacemakers?

The word for peacemaker is *eirēnopoios:* the two parts of this word being *eirēnē* – "peace, quietness, and rest", and *poiēo* "bring, cause, exercise, gain, give, hold, keep, make, provide". Put them together, and we get something like, *"cause peace, make quietness, bring or provide rest and peace."* While not necessarily denoting total absence of trouble, *eirēnē* "is everything that makes for our highest good."[30] It is more than a quality though, since this one also involves action. *Eirēnopoios* or "peacemaker" ("maker of *eirēnē* or peace, also translated "quietness" as in Acts 24:2), according to Vine,[31] involves:

- Harmonious relationships between men
- Harmonious relationships between nations
- Friendliness (hence a peacemaker will be a friendly person!)
- Freedom from molestation, and therefore safety

30   Barclay, Ibid, p. 148
31   pp. 841-842

- Order in the state
- Order in the churches
- The harmonised relationship between God and man, accomplished through the gospel . . . so consequently
- Rest and contentment

A peacemaker, then, is a friendly person—safe and contented—who helps others to be the same. According to Strong, there is an implication of genuine personal as well as communal prosperity in this concept of peace, quietness, and rest. We must ourselves make our peace with God, with others, and with our communities.

It is the antithesis of what is forbidden in the commandment, "Thou shalt not kill". In other words, life is precious and important—both ours and others'. Peacemaking is enhancing and preserving life by settling arguments and solving conflicts; hence, it is fulfilling the command to value life. Peacemaking needs people who have both mercy and purity of heart. It needs people who will *cause peace, make quietness, and bring or provide rest and peace*. Every believer can pray for peace, and in this way, be a peacemaker. The world we live in needs an unending number of active peacemakers to serve in that capacity, and this will be true as long as there are humans living on the earth. These peacemakers do not shy away from issues. They are realists, and they face issues with the faith, wisdom, and resolve that only God can give. They are also willing to handle the inevitable opposition.

Peacemaking has many facets, but at its heart is the fact that by making our peace with God, we can then help others make their peace with God. Forgiveness is unilateral. We give it, or God gives it, and someone receives it. Reconciliation requires two or more parties to come together. It is bilateral, and multilateral. It's all about making right relationships and bringing people together.

Secondly, by seeing conflicts between people or groups and being able to mediate and bring reconciliation and agreement, we can fulfil Christ's command to love. Bringing a truce between warring parties in a regional or international conflict is certainly peacemaking in one sense, but peacemaking can also be a normal part of our Christian practice.

We have seen the qualities, and now we see the practice. Peacemaking is active. It is going out of our way to help others. It is not sticking your nose into other people's business or being unwise. There is a proverb that states that meddling with strife that doesn't belong to you is like grabbing a dog by its ears (Proverbs 26:17), which is not a particularly wise thing to do. We have to leave some situations alone, or give them to the experts such as the police, the law, or other legitimate authorities, but none of these can fulfil the first function of peacemaking (and the *only* function for those for whom the other roles are impractical or beyond their ability), which is helping others to be at peace with God. This is indeed a believer's privilege, and all other types of peacemaking are, for believers in Christ, outflows from lives lived in humble service to the One who will ultimately reconcile all things to Himself.

God is a reconciler, and so you can be too in all kinds of situations. Mediation, negotiation, intercession, reconciliation—these are the calling of every believer to some extent or other, but fulfilling this beatitude requires wisdom and love. In fact, it requires (and we should know the list by now) poverty of spirit, a heart prepared to grieve and mourn over sin and over a world that God cares for, meekness, true righteousness, mercy, and purity. Take any of these out of the equation, and at best, we'll be struggling, and at worst, we might actually contribute to the problem, hinder the resolution, or become victims of the conflict we are trying to solve. This applies to bringing people to peace with God too; the qualities which are to be the model for the believer must be there with sincerity for there to be any success. The peace of a person's soul is the only issue we can be absolutely sure we believers can "meddle" with; again, it is every true Christian's business, even if it is only to pray for someone or for a situation.

Do not expect everyone to love you the minute you start out peacemaking. That's obviously not going to happen, as we shall see, because the very next beatitude is about being persecuted for the sake of righteousness. People will hate you for being so "right", let alone so "righteous". You will be called all kinds of things, and in this context, told that it is not your business, so you had better be sure that it *is* your business and that peace in their soul is your ultimate aim.

PERSECUTION

"Blessed are they which are persecuted for righteousness' sake:
for theirs is the kingdom of heaven."

Objection*: "Why get yourself into trouble needlessly? Just go with the general melee of what's popular and accept it. Christians are nerds and deserve what they get! People who are really genuinely being unjustly persecuted should fight back! Crush the opposition, and do it with vengeance and determination. If someone smites you on one cheek, smash them on both of theirs!"*

Response: Christians have always been persecuted, so it is nothing new to the church. It is generally considered an honour to suffer for the sake of the Saviour, to be ostracised for doing the right thing, so long as we know it is the right thing. "Let none of you suffer as a murderer, or as a thief, or as an evildoer, or as a busybody in other men's matters. Yet, if any man suffer as a Christian [Christianos – "a partisan of Christ"], let him not be ashamed; but let him glorify God on this behalf [i.e., "in that name"]" (1 Peter 4:15-16). Vengeance and revenge just recycle hatred, and sometimes it can snowball and affect large numbers of people. Forgiveness of those who have wronged us, as well as those who accuse us falsely, is an essential part of a Christian's life. Accusation and opposition happened to Jesus, so we should not be surprised if it happens to us sometimes. Going against the flow for the right reason develops character, even if you are not a believer, as long as you have the right reaction and maintain perspective. However, it is hard to bear without the love of God to guide and comfort and without the supernatural power of the Holy Spirit to help you to forgive. Although self-defence from tyrants and criminals is everyone's right, having enemies for the sake of the gospel is normal for the Christian.

This follows on from peacemaking in one sense because although the peace may have been established, the problem-maker may now want to persecute the peacemaker. This can sometimes be one unavoidable source of persecution, but there are others.

The key words here are "for righteousness' sake". This is the only acceptable persecution from God's perspective, and it was the only reason that Jesus was persecuted and eventually crucified. Those who hated Him were opposed to His righteousness and His message of their need for true righteousness from God and not their own *self*-righteousness. It was all to do with His stand for what was right and true, for that exposed their sin and unrighteousness. It was said of Him that "He is despised and rejected of men" (Isaiah 53:3a) as a result of this stand.

Many people and groups talk about the persecution they receive from here and there. Some sect has separated itself from society and then complains of persecution for some reason. Most of the time the reason is immaterial, the claim bogus, the "righteousness" phony—self-righteous being the better term. These groups hunker down and separate themselves even more in their ivory towers or their little communities, claiming victimhood and further confirming their own thinking that the world is against them because of their beliefs. Most of the time, it's not true. However, there are some, and throughout history, many, who can legitimately say so. Read *Foxe's Book of Martyrs*, Richard Wurmbrand's *Sermons in Solitary Confinement*, or the works of Alexander Solzhenitsyn. Persecution has been real and vicious, as well as subversive and subtle over the centuries. Individuals, nations, and groups have been hounded for various reasons. In this beatitude, Jesus is speaking of a specific persecution—that which is for righteousness' sake—for living righteously, for doing righteously, and for standing for righteousness. This brings us back to the opening promise given to the poor in spirit: that *theirs* is the kingdom of heaven.

The kingdom of heaven is for the poor in spirit, and it is for the persecuted.

The eighth beatitude is the only one Jesus personalised and expanded on. He could have finished with verse 10, but here it would seem that those who are truly and consistently *all* of those things that are mentioned in the first seven beatitudes will be persecuted. Now He says, "Blessed are you".

This then becomes the ninth beatitude.

> "Blessed are ye, when *men* shall revile you, and persecute *you*, and shall say all manner of evil against you falsely for my sake. Rejoice, and be exceeding glad: for great *is* your reward in heaven: for so persecuted they the prophets which were before you." Matthew 5:11-12

"Blessed are ye . . . you . . . *you* . . . you . . . your . . . you." The focus is now firmly on those sitting there on that hill two thousand years ago. It is now personal. This was also prophetic, as it is what they would experience not that much later. Where it seems up till then that Jesus was making a wider sweep with His statements, "Blessed are they", it is now clear that this is what He also naturally expected of His disciples. He is saying that this is what will happen; this is how they will react; and here is the reason why they will react in that way. By implication, it applies to all those over time who are truly His followers.

There are two words used here that are similar. First, "rejoice"—*chairō*—which means "calmly happy or well-off" (Strong), in the sense of being "cheerful". It is derived from *chára* which means "joy, delight, gladness" and of course *cháris* "grace", and is synonymous to a degree with the second set of words, "be exceeding glad", which are summed up in a more intense phrase, namely *agalliáō*, "to exult, rejoice greatly". The latter speaks of skipping or leaping with joy and indicates "excessive or ecstatic joy and delight", often connected with song and dance in its use in the Septuagint (Greek translation) of the Old Testament. So, "Rejoice—*chairō*, i.e., have a quiet, calm contentment over the matter, and "be exceeding glad"—*agalliáō*, i.e., literally jump for joy and rejoice with singing and dancing, two words cast in the imperative in contrast with all the descriptive comments that have come before in this passage. Simply, "because of all that you are and what will result from it, be cheerful and joyful!"

There are degrees of persecution, and the word in the English language is normally reserved for the more extreme type of opposition that anyone may get for their stand on a particular matter. However, in the Christian experience worldwide, it is common, whether in its mild, moderate, or extreme forms. Below are examples of all three.

The first is the mild form which many new Christians will experience in some form or another. I will take a simple example from my own experience. When I first became a Christian in 1978-9 at the age of 21, I was travelling in the United States and Canada. My real commitment to Jesus came after I left the USA and went to Canada. My uncle in the USA had given me a New Testament, and I began to get into the Word of God in earnest. On the train from Toronto to Vancouver, I got food poisoning and was sick for a few days. I decided to fast for seven days. At that time, I was staying with someone who took exception to my newfound enthusiasm for Jesus and made it clear I was no longer welcome to stay with them. This person did help me to find new accommodation, and this turned out to be on campus at the University of British Columbia. There, I met a former Hell's Angel biker who had been converted to Christ and was studying theology. He connected me with some other students also studying theology, and I attended several lectures with them, and this started me on a lifelong love of biblical study and theology. He also suggested some helpful resources, which I bought and still use now.

The initial opposition to my faith actually worked to bring me closer to God and to a stronger faith. This is what sometimes happens with resistance. It strengthens our resolve and our commitment and can become an opportunity for God to reveal Himself to us.

The second is the stronger type of resistance, which is more common to those who come from a background where Christianity is treated with either disdain or suspicion and where the pressure on a new believer is greater than what others may experience. Not long before writing this, my wife and I were privileged to meet and be invited into the life of a young woman from a non-Western background who was just discovering for herself what real faith in Christ Jesus meant. Many a Sunday morning, she would quietly leave the house to come to church with us. When her relatives learned she was doing this, they deliberately planned to block her from going. This continued for many months, and sometimes her efforts were sabotaged. However, they underestimated her persistence and determination, and she never gave up at least trying to go to church, even when it was obvious that she would only encounter more anger and resistance. Finally, she met a good Christian man of her own culture and got married, and they are now joyfully serving God together.

Now, for the most extreme persecution. This type is never pleasant to read about and does not always have a happy ending, at least in the physical world. Here is a story about a believer in a particular nation who was arrested in 2004. I will quote from my source: "She was severely beaten in an effort to break her faith and was kept in a metal shipping container in the desert for extended periods with up to twenty others, enduring stifling heat, bitter cold, and disease." Over twenty containers were used in this way, and up to 400 prisoners were kept in them and routinely tortured. The person concerned wrote, "I can not [sic] believe that this is my life . . . these four metal walls, all of us corralled like cattle, the pain, the hunger, the fear. All because of my belief in a God who is risen, who charges me to share my faith with those who do not yet know him, and who I am forbidden to worship." Her crime?

She was a gospel singer and had released an album of Christian music. In this case, due to international pressure, the woman was released and given asylum in a Western country.[32] I recently read of a North Korean pastor who was not so fortunate. He was hacked to death for his efforts to share the love of God with others. For those like him—and the list is in the millions for the last one hundred years, let alone the past two thousand years—his *makarios* (blessing) was not one to be found on this earth, but in heaven.

It will be helpful here to venture ahead briefly into the body of the Sermon on the Mount to see what Jesus said our reaction should be to those who persecute, hate, or curse us—whether such dislike is mild, moderate, or extreme. We find the famous words in verses 43 to 47 in this same fifth chapter of Matthew:

> "Love your enemies, bless them that curse you, do good to them
> that hate you, and pray for them which despitefully use you, and
> persecute you" (v. 44).

It is not enough to just forgive, but we must also love, bless, do good, and pray. This is a formula designed for our benefit, as well as theirs should they choose to receive it. In fact, our enemy might go on to make conflict with others, pillaging and bullying their way through life, committing offenses left and right. They may move on from one victim to another and have probably forgotten all about us, while we are still stewing about them. Here's the catch: if you don't forgive them, then it is you that suffers, and it may be you, *more* than them, who suffers at the present moment because you are the one who is affected by it. So, the formula God gives is for *your* benefit, for *your* blessing, and it is quite clear: forgive and do not retaliate—*love, bless, do good,* and *pray* for them.[33]

Someone I was involved with once over a certain matter had been particularly difficult about it and had caused me a lot of stress. A few weeks later, my wife

---

32   *Voice of the Martyrs,* Jan/Feb 2010
33   Studies have shown that simply going out and doing a good deed for someone helps lower blood pressure.

read in the news that this person had been arrested for a crime. Initially, I felt a satisfaction that they had gotten their comeuppance, and I gloated inwardly. However, I woke up that same night with the awareness that something was wrong. Feeling stressed and unsettled, I immediately knew what the problem was. There and then, I forgave them and prayed for them. My conscience had spoken, yet it was more than just a human matter. It was a clear sense of the "voice" of God speaking into my heart: "Forgive and you will be forgiven."

> "For he is kind to the unthankful and *to* the evil. Be ye therefore
> merciful, as your Father also is merciful" (Luke 6:35d, 36).

There is another verse of Scripture which is given to us both in the Old Testament in Proverbs, and in the New Testament in Romans. It is essentially the same in both instances. "If thine enemy hunger, feed him; if he thirst, give him drink: for in so doing thou shalt heap coals of fire on his head" (Romans 12:20; Proverbs 25:21-22). The last part of this verse is an idiom in the traditional languages that could be paraphrased as follows: "by heaping good deeds onto your enemy, your enemy then becomes ashamed and is prompted to cease rewarding you evil for good, and is provoked by his or her own conscience to make peace and be kind to others as well."

A great example of this is found in the story of the king of Syria warring against Israel, besieging Dothan to try to capture Elisha the prophet, and then being led himself unwittingly with his armies into Samaria—straight to his arch-enemy, the king of Israel (2 Kings 6:8-23). The king of Israel is then dissuaded by Elisha from killing all the Syrians and instead is advised to feed them and send them back to their leader. As a result, we are told that "the bands of Syria came no more into the land of Israel" (v. 23). Israel had fed their enemy and the marauding bands of Syrians had been put to shame. So, they stopped their aggression. Here is an example of mercy extended from Israel to Syria.

Enemies exist or emerge quite naturally, and it's logical that one must have one in order to love one. While nobody naturally wants enemies, Jesus expected that His followers would have at least some. He spoke as if it was a given. It's also better not to have too many, and no one will be disappointed if they have too few, but we ought to be worried if we have none, because that would indicate that we have stood for nothing. If all men speak well of us, it could be an indication of a lack on our part.

"Woe unto you, when all men shall speak well of you!" (Luke 6:26)

But what kind of love is this that we should have? It cannot be the same as a love for our family members or friends, which is a natural heart response. Neither can it be the same as passionate love, as what one would have for one's spouse. In fact, those are described with very different words in the Greek of the New Testament. A unique form of the word is used here when discussing our enemies: *agapan*, found throughout the New Testament, particularly in 1 Corinthians 13, and which William Barclay explains below:[34]

> *Agapan* describes an active feeling of benevolence towards the other person; it means that no matter what that person does to us we will never allow ourselves to desire anything but his highest good; and we will deliberately and of set purpose go out of our way to be good and kind to him . . . We cannot love our enemies as we love our nearest and dearest. To do so would be unnatural, impossible and even wrong. But we can see to it that, no matter what a man does to us, even if he insults, ill-treats and injures us, we will seek nothing but his highest good.

Agapan or *agape* love is God's love, and the Beatitudes are an expression of the love of God at work in us. It flows with the *makarios*—the blessing. In particular relevance to this are the two verses in 1 Peter where in the KJV the word "happy" is used for *makarios*.

"If ye suffer for righteousness' sake, happy *are ye*" (3:14), and "If ye be reproached for the name of Christ, happy *are ye*" (4:14).

Makarios has the sense of "beautify", hence the "beatitudes". According to scholar Kenneth Wuest[35], a former teacher in New Testament Greek at

34   1975, p. 78
35   Wuest, 1945, p. 76

Moody Bible Institute, "The fact that these saints [i.e., the ones in Asia Minor who Peter was writing to in the first century] were being persecuted, was an indication that they were in a happy or prosperous condition spiritually."

Though he speaks of spiritual prosperity, it does remind us also of what John wrote to Gaius, probably not too long after Peter had written his letters: "Beloved, I wish above all things that thou mayest prosper and be in health, even as thy soul prospereth" (3 John 1:2). The term "prosper" here means "good progress, help along the road, success in reaching somewhere, in the sense also of having success in business affairs or having a prosperous journey". The word in question, *ĕŭŏdŏō*, is translated similarly four times, coming from *eu*—"well", and *hodos*—"way or road". Both words describe the kind of "happiness" or blessedness promised in the Beatitudes.

Finally, in this look at persecution and Jesus's promises, it can be noted that most of the time opposition requires such a response as that given above, the offering of the other cheek which makes for peace, the opposite of "an eye for an eye, and a tooth for a tooth" (Matthew 5:38-41), which is really another way of being a peacemaker; however, self-defence is still legitimate in certain contexts and Scripture has some advice about it since there are valid times to resist earthly powers, but not in ways that contradict our roles as believers. There are also times to resist *spiritual* powers, as sometimes physical opposition may yet be the result of a certain spiritual stance, and Satan stirs up opposition from all quarters at times, both physical and spiritual. Even our own emotions may at times contradict what we know is good and right. In some cases, this could be outward evidence of spiritual forces working in opposition against us—proof of "war in the heavenlies". God fights for us in these instances. However, we also must resist in the spirit by fervent prayer and, if necessary, fasting. "Resist the devil, and he will flee from you" (James 4:7). This is spiritual self-defence, not forgetting the need at times for spiritually *offensive* action, e.g., strategically-targeted prayer.

God also never asks us to lie down and submit to an intimidator, a robber, or someone who threatens our life or that of our fellow humans and loved ones. Here, there is a need for a different approach. Proverbs 25:26 says, "A righteous man falling down before the wicked *is as* a troubled fountain, and a corrupt spring". What this means is that we should not "fall down" ("waver, slip, or shake") in front of a wicked person out of fear of them. There is no fear in love, and at times, a rebuke or a path of resistance can be timely and appropriate. Would you protect your children? Your wife? Your best friend? Would you run away or would you fight for them if need be and if you could? Naturally, the latter would be the case for most people.

If at all possible, we are to live peaceably with everyone, but *sometimes* we must either deliberately avoid or even resist someone with evil intent who is threatening us or those near us. Some of these people are quite different from overt enemies of the gospel, and are difficult people no matter who they are dealing with. The formula given in Matthew in dealing with difficult people is still the same in one sense: to make every attempt to *forgive, love, bless, do good,* and *pray for* them as you would your enemies. There are times, however, when a show of strength from somewhere is necessary; indeed, a very different type of "laying on of hands"! Otherwise, why bother with a police force? In the environment we live in, there is no reason why normal measures of protection should not be taken.

It is possible that attacks come as our spiritual enemy finds chinks in our spiritual armour, perhaps even a besetting sin, both of which can leave us exposed spiritually or physically. This aside, there is nothing wrong with a believer learning how to defend themselves in a corrupt and violent society, or, for example, when they travel. Even legally carrying a firearm in certain parts of the world may, in certain circumstances, be necessary. When I was growing up in New Zealand, it was not uncommon to go out and leave the doors unlocked, but not so now. And currently, in places such as parts of South Africa, people sometimes need suitable weaponry to stay safe, regardless of whether they are Christian or not. On the other hand, if you live in a comfortable society, but believe in never defending yourself, why would you even bother to lock your door?

Jesus once advised His disciples to sell their garments and buy a sword (Luke 22:36). It was not that He wanted them to be aggressive and warlike, but rather because He was aware of their impending change of circumstances. Whereas before He took care of their needs and protected them, after He was gone they would soon need a "scrip" (a bag for holding provisions), a "purse" (a money container), and a short sword or knife which could be used for all kinds of practical purposes and, if necessary, for protection from wild animals or robbers.[36]

Jesus was saying that the disciples would have to fend for themselves for a time after He was gone. Their coming need for self-provision and self-defence was quite possibly the focus of Jesus's words here. His disciples then said to Him, "here are two swords" and He replied, "It is enough". Perhaps He was really saying, "You may not be using them in the way that you are thinking—you haven't quite got the purpose yet!" In verse 47 of Matthew 26, it says that a "great multitude" came to get him "with swords and staves" (v. 52), against which two swords were hardly a match! Peter, as usual, got it wrong still further, pulling out his sword and cutting off one of the chief priest's servant's ears as they came to arrest Jesus. He wanted to make a point and show them some steel, and was probably also trying to demonstrate his loyalty to Jesus, even though he knew that it wouldn't be much use against the determined forces arrayed against them. He could be admired for having a certain amount of fearlessness, yet Jesus gave him some perspective with His words: "Put up again thy sword into his place, for all that take the sword shall perish with the sword"[37] (Matthew 26:52). Peter was trying to resist

---

36 Much as the Gurkhas in places like Sikkim and Darjeeling even now sometimes carry a kukri knife with them for normal everyday purposes such as cutting firewood, but only if absolutely necessary for self-protection from others.

37 Note that carrying a sword appears to have been fairly commonplace then since the disciples had at least two, and this was not questioned or discouraged, but rather the wrong use of it.

Jesus's persecutors and in this case "resist not evil" (Matthew 5:39) was the application. Jesus Himself exemplified His own words in the Sermon on the Mount, given some three years earlier, to "bless them that . . . persecute you", by now *healing* one of His enemies on the spot by restoring the severed ear.[38] Yet Jesus was the one with the most cause to cry "unjust!"

His words implied that a lifestyle of violent resistance was even further from the way He had taught and would end up in disaster. Peter did not have a mandate to violently resist on Jesus's behalf. Even though the multitude coming to put Jesus to trial was far more like a lynch mob than respectable representatives of legitimate authority, resisting would have been seen by many as being seditious. Ultimately, in this case, Peter had to realise that it was God who was in charge, even though things seemed to be going differently from what he had expected.

As long as we are not being persecuted for our own folly and lack of wisdom, we can follow the guidance from Scripture on how to handle persecution, but to stand up against political oppression or unjust laws (not necessarily to take up arms!), or to stand in a court for truth and justice or to defend the weak and vulnerable in society, or to defend a constitutional right, all these are the Christian's prerogative as with anyone else. People in politics and law, including those of faith, have to stick up for what they believe regardless of how others react. However, the Christian person is to always deal honourably with enemies while resisting malicious evildoers and madmen who threaten the overall safety of society. In summary then, there is a time to defend oneself and there is a time to refrain from doing so. We need to make sure that we know the difference!

Finally, whether in times of persecution or simply in difficult times where safety is an issue, there are always the mighty assurances of God's Word that He is in control and that He will deliver His people. It may not always be as we wish, but it is good for us in those uncertain times to take courage, strength,

---

38   Thus also preventing Peter from getting into serious trouble.

and confidence from promises such as those of Psalm 91 and throughout Scripture where God's presence and protection is expressed. This is especially applicable when our foes are spiritual or inspired by evil spiritual forces. In the aforementioned psalm, God says wonderful statements such as "He shall cover thee with his feathers" and "there shall no evil befall thee". It is a good idea to commit to memory some of these psalms and other similar Scriptures. They will always prove to be a comfort, encouragement, and hope in times of trial of any kind, including trials of opposition to our faith.

So to sum up the last three beatitudes, they are the three "p"s: peacemaking, persecution, and—again—persecution.

PRESENT DAY APPLICATION

We need to realise that keeping the Beatitudes close to our heart and at the forefront of our experience is part of our worship of God. They help us to be like the One who spoke them. Those who worship God in spirit and in truth should be more Christlike as they progress through their lives. This is part of what the Beatitudes are about. However, they who worship false gods become like those gods (Psalm 115:8, 135:18). False gods are always false—they never magically become true, whether they are the false idols of Western materialism or the world's false religious gods which are untrustworthy and capricious.[39] There are personal and societal consequences of not honouring these truths. Yet there has also been great benefit given to those societies that *have* honoured them, and this is discussed further here.

Trustworthiness in relationships and in business has in the past been at the core of much of Western culture, and where it has been weakened or undermined, it is due to the effects of sin. In some places in the world, it is not even found in the general vocabulary, although there may be some synonyms. People are naturally suspicious of others, and all or most dealings are done with an air of distrust. Indeed, when gods which cannot be trusted are worshiped, so their devotees start to resemble them.

Trustworthiness, on the other hand, stems from the belief—the firm conviction of the truth—that God the Creator is Himself dependable and that His word is sure. Those who truly follow Him then start to *become* like Him

---

39 Note also that God says that He "sets His face" against those who make idols in their *heart* (see Ezekiel 14:8).

and expect that the lies that others speak be minimised or eliminated, and that all dealings in relationships and business be towards, and not away from, the basis of trust. If we take this away, we end up with an untamed society which ultimately becomes an inferior one, because as everyone does what is right in their own eyes so relationships and business dealings become weakened and subject to the corruption of men's sins. The result is breakdown, stress, strife, wrong decisions, corruption, bribery, control where there should be freedom, laxity where there should be control, and failure to achieve all that is good and peaceful. Life is reduced to a "dog-eat-dog" existence, or else solely to an obligation-based society of reciprocal relationships in which it is all about you doing something for me and then me (under obligation) doing something for you. Both approaches tend to create distrust and grudging dutifulness at best and, at worst, increasing hardness and cruelty, after which society becomes ruled by raw power alone.

It goes without saying that an untamed society cannot produce the type of relationships that flow from an honest attempt to abide by the Beatitudes and the laws of God, for these have over time contributed to the concept of contracts and agreements being sacrosanct. The idea that "your word is your bond" has developed wherever God's Word has been respected as an unchangeable, inviolable covenant. *His* word is *His* bond, and therefore those who follow Him follow His example. God is reliable to do what He says and perform what He promises, honouring His commitments and keeping His word. In short, He is a gentleman, and He makes "gentleman's agreements".

The Bible has been the most prominent book of all in Western culture, albeit the most controversial and most challenged. Because this knowledge has been extant for millennia it has become a part of our psyche and a sacrosanct aspect of many of our traditional political, legal, and business structures.[40] Naturally, this does not mean that it is never contradicted in these structures or in personal dealings, as we all have sinful natures, and

---

40   Common law, for example, was originally strongly influenced by it.

we all transgress at times, but it remains as a set of principles and values which we still hold dear.

In contrast, where capricious or overbearing dictatorships exist side by side with "do what thou wilt" philosophies, people tend to blunder along and plunder from others, and millions suffer the adverse effects. If a community is *only* about what it can get and how it can survive, then all kinds of dodgy shortcuts and crossing of boundaries are permitted, and integrity and principles go out the window.

Those who have the Beatitudes at heart, who have these principles and concepts at work by the grace of God in their lives, are like salt and light in society. Light is necessary for everything to live, and is the antithesis of darkness; this is what we are to be. The earth is like a big dish of food needing salt to flavour it. Salt is effective in large amounts, such as when it surrounds meat to preserve it, and it is also useful in small amounts for baking and flavouring. It also eats into things and helps clean out dirt, used as an agent in cleaners of various kinds. It is unpleasant if it gets into your eyes or into a cut, but it also helps to heal. Our world has multiple cuts and wounds, and those who follow the Beatitudes will sometimes be like salt in the wounds—hence the persecution—yet ultimately with a beneficial effect. They "deal truly" (Ezekiel 18:9) and are trustworthy; they are humble, and at times, pacify strife as peacemakers in the world. They uphold the laws of God and portray them clearly by their righteousness and mercy. At the heart of it is the life of God in individual believers and in their societies, where freedom is respected because responsibility is expected.

SUMMARY

Jesus forgave us a debt that we could not pay (Matthew 18:24-27). As a result, we love Him by being poor in spirit, willing to mourn over that which grieves God's Spirit, willing to be meek, to hunger and thirst for righteousness, to be pure in heart, merciful, peacemakers, and to endure opposition. Here is the kingdom of heaven, comfort, inheritance, contact with and vision of God, mercy, and rejoicing, and its root is grace.

Note the two uses of the kingdom (*basileia*) of heaven (or the kingdom of God as it is in Luke and the other Gospels).

- The sphere of God's rule on earth now, albeit with some suffering for righteousness' sake
- The future reward for the righteous

According to Jesus's teachings, it is not only faith that counts. It is also what we do, as seen in the previous notes on the fourth beatitude. Who you are is important; you are what God made you, but He can also *re*-make you. The *be*-ing is just the beginning! There is work to do.

Just like Matthew, Zacchaeus was a publican (a despised tax-collector). He was accepted by Jesus for what he promised to do because it was evidence of his change of heart (Luke 19:1-10). He was like the publican in the previous chapter (Luke 18:13), who beat his breast and said, "God, be merciful to me a sinner". In line with the legal requirements of the Mosaic covenant (as, for example, in Leviticus 6:1-5), Zacchaeus promised to give half of his possessions to the poor, and to restore fourfold anything he may have taken by false accusation, which was the amount required from a sheep-stealer to be recompensed to their victim (Exodus 22:1). For Zacchaeus's response to what was required by the law, Jesus said to him, "This day is salvation come to this house" (Luke 19:9), in accordance with Ezekiel 33:15-16.[41]

This day then, salvation must come to our house, too. If the law of God was good enough for Jesus to use in resisting His and our greatest spiritual foe, Satan, then it is good enough for us also to know, to memorise, and to allow God to apply in our lives through His Spirit. The law was the basis for these beatitudes; however, it was to lead to so much more. A new and living

---

41 "*If* the wicked restore the pledge, give again that he had robbed, walk in the statutes of life, without committing iniquity; he shall surely live, he shall not die. None of his sins that he hath committed shall be mentioned unto him: he hath done that which is lawful and right; he shall surely live."

way was inaugurated by the Lord in these ten simple statements in Matthew 5:3-12: a way that led to an astounding new revelation and understanding of the dealings between God and His people. It was a way of faith and a way to live in the power of a salvation by faith, which would enable all who embrace it to rise above mere legal ritual alone to a life of spiritual power and love. This could only ever be instigated by a sacrifice far greater than lambs and goats and heifers, a sacrifice that only God Himself could make, whereby our sins would be forever forgiven and our lives forever changed by His gift of the Holy Spirit in our hearts.

The Beatitudes are about things far deeper, grander, longer-lasting, and worthwhile than the trivia we often engage with in our daily lives. Deeper issues are at stake, such as how we react when things don't go our way, and how we conduct our daily lives in the more essential, eternal issues which affect every man, woman, and child on the planet. They address how we begin our character development as young people, behave ourselves in middle life in work, relationships, and ministry, and how we end our lives—with grace and graciousness or with a negative view of life which is directly opposite to these wonderful "positive-attitude" producing, glorious statements from God, as given to us by the Lord Jesus Christ.

When Jesus gave this message, He was living in a society and a world where the concepts He taught were being disregarded in many respects, a state we can relate to today. From that perspective, some might say, "Well, why bother?" That, however, is to give up all hope and to offer no solution. Jesus's ministry was to *restore* hope and bring salvation to as many as would hear and receive His message. It was a hope and a salvation in which fulfilment of these ethics was possible, but what could be the consequences of deliberately disregarding or discarding them? In Luke 6:24-26, Jesus illustrated this by putting them in the reverse.

> But woe unto you that are rich! for ye have received your consolation [or comfort]. Woe unto you that are full! for ye shall

hunger. Woe unto you that laugh now! for ye shall mourn and weep. Woe unto you, when all men shall speak well of you! for so did their fathers to the false prophets.

Here are negatives to the first, fourth, second, and ninth beatitudes of Matthew's gospel. The first woe is probably not metaphorical in its reference to rich since the word is mainly used positively in the New Testament, e.g., "rich in faith" (of believers), and "rich in mercy" (of God), with only one usage in the negative, in Revelation 3:17: "Because thou sayest, I am rich, and increased with goods, and have need of nothing." Therefore, it probably means those who are literally rich or who at least *think* they are rich.

So in Luke's passage above, there is a clear distinction made between the person of faith and the indulgent over-prosperous who will not acknowledge God, like the rich man and Lazarus. We have seen that Matthew was speaking of poverty *of spirit* rather than actual physical poverty, but the two can be harmonised, just as "full" in Luke refers more to religious smugness, which ultimately leads to "hunger", and "laugh" refers to carelessness of spiritual needs which ultimately leads to "mourning" and "weeping".[42] In Matthew's account, the Beatitudes could perhaps be reversed something like this[43]:

> Cursed are the haughty in spirit, for they cannot enter the kingdom of God.

> Cursed are those who cannot mourn, for they shall be comfortless.

> Cursed are the proud, for their days shall be short and they will be left without inheritance.

---

42   The last woe has already been discussed in the previous chapter; "all men speaking well of you" being a likely indication that you are *not* in the right place with God! "Friendship with the world is enmity with God" – and, since the reverse also applies, there will always be resistance and opposition to those who do what's right, particularly those who proclaim God's Word.

43   Indeed, in the 23rd chapter of Matthew, the eight themes of the Beatitudes are hinted at, in order, in the eight "woes" which Jesus delivers to the Pharisees who did the opposite to what the Beatitudes required. Compare each of these verses (13, 14, 15, 16-22, 23 & 24, 25 & 26, 27 & 28, 29-33) with, respectively, verses 3, 4, 5, 6, 7, 8, 9, 10-12 in chapter five.

Cursed are the unrighteous, for they shall remain empty.

Cursed are the unmerciful, for they shall not receive mercy.

Cursed are the impure in heart, for they shall never see God.

Cursed are the warmongers, for they are the children of the evil one.

Cursed are they who are never persecuted due to their never standing up for what is right and true, for they cannot enter the kingdom of heaven.

So now you can say that you have read a book on the Beatitudes! You might make one of several choices at this point. You might do nothing or you might reject it all because you are not yet fully convinced of its relevance for today or of its attainability. Perhaps, though, you have already started on the journey to making them real in your life. If that is true, then it is quite likely that sooner or later someone close to you is going to pipe up and say something like, "OK, so let's see it in action!" What they mean, or perhaps just think, is what you'd expect: "Where's the meekness? Where's the purity? Where's the mercy?"

They may be right. It's nice to read a book and learn a few Greek words and mull over some of the ideas, but . . . well, let's see it all in action!

That brings us to the choice that we all need to make, to choose whether or not to specifically pray that the qualities described in Matthew chapter 5 will become a reality in our lives. This is also a prayer for a right relationship with God, to receive Jesus in your heart, for mercy in your life, for love for God and for your neighbour (which covers everything, your neighbour being the *person next to you*—at home, in the traffic, at work, on the street, at your place of worship). If you haven't got that love, and you know you need it, then perhaps right now, as you read this, you could get on your knees or just sit silently in a quiet place or with a trusted friend or prayer partner, and pray for it.

The Beatitudes are not impossible and were never intended to be hypothetical, only for two thousand years ago, only for "saints" in isolated communities, or for some kind of special person. Rather, they can be fleshed out each day and can become habitual ways of thinking. Although they often go against the grain of our human nature and can be contrary to our earthly experience and the trends of our societies where selfishness, pride, cruelty, and retaliation are so common, they still remain the only way to truly honour our Creator.

It is the same challenge that we face—that I face—to fulfil them, but with the infilling and indwelling of the Spirit of God, it is possible. It is *necessary,* both for our faith and for the formation of any truly caring community. There is no age restriction on it; it's for all, but the Beatitudes do not come automatically to us, neither do they come just by reading them. They need to be imparted and worked into our lives by the power of our Creator, and then worked *out* in our lives on a daily basis. The place to start is prayer.

I invite you to make a prayer along these lines:

God, I need to be poor in spirit. Help me to experience what you mean by "the kingdom of heaven".

Help me to mourn over the right things and to experience your comfort.

Help me to be meek and to have the right relationship with you—to "inherit the earth", whatever that might mean for me.

Help me to hunger and thirst for real righteousness, not my own self-righteousness, and to know what it is to be filled by you.

Help me to be merciful and to experience your mercy.

Help me to be pure in heart and to know what it is to "see" you, to perceive you and your ways.

Help me to be a peacemaker and to have the assurance that I am your child, that I might be called "a child of God".

Help me to have the resilience to face opposition in the right attitude and to be able to rejoice and be glad whenever that takes place. In facing trouble or persecution help me to have the strength to always stand for what is right.

Empower me, Lord, that I may have these qualities formed in me.

Amen.

Following this, you might also pray a "beatitude prayer" that those in your household, your neighbourhood, your place of worship, your city, and your nation, would also begin to desire these qualities. While a nation or a group of people can have them as a shared set of reference points and values, a person seeking to serve God must have them all functional, or at least in the process of being formed, before they can be used by God. Of course, God can sovereignly use anyone for His overall purpose since He can, and often does, overrule everything, but the vessel He will *consistently* use to minister *effectively* to the needs of the world and to His people must have the Beatitudes operational in their life.

So, going through them one by one, pray that people would:

- Become "beggars for the principle of life"
- Mourn over sin and wrongdoing
- Be meek in spirit and humble in heart while also strong in integrity
- Be hungry and thirsty for righteousness
- Be merciful in all their dealings
- Be pure, having a clear focus of their calling and purpose
- Be peacemakers, leading people to the God of peace as well as actively making peace in their family and community
- Be able to endure persecution for their commitment to these things, and to do so with the right attitude

My prayer is that the Beatitudes will become a reality to all who read them.

It was noted in the Introduction to this book that the Sermon was on "a mount". For us, perhaps Jesus is also on a "mountain", where we have to make an effort to climb up to meet Him if we want to learn anything. Going up any hill or mountain takes some effort. He may have been on the top, the side, or only half-way up, but His disciples had to go up that mountain to meet him. For us now, this may mean the effort we make to read, study, and memorise His life and teachings, and the quest to actually practise His sayings.

The Beatitudes take around twelve seconds to speed-read, about twenty-five seconds to read in detail, and about forty-five seconds to recite. It's so easy to read them quickly and pass over them lightly with little understanding of what they are really about.

They formed the basis and the beginning of all that Jesus taught as well as all the subsequent moral teachings of the New Testament.

They are the highest of all moral teachings and as such deserve to be memorised and studied in detail. They ought to be taught in every religious institution on the planet. At the very least, the first six of them should be taught in every school and every institution of higher learning, and written on the hearts of those in positions of political power and influence. They also should be preached regularly in every pulpit, and every culture, regardless of their beliefs, has a right to hear about them.

They, along with their exposition and fulfilment throughout the Scriptures, have changed many people over the centuries and will continue to change people everywhere.

And they will continue to bring radical personal and corporate transformation to any community or nation which adopts and applies them.

NOTES ON THE ORDER OF THE BEATITUDES

Firstly, when read and considered as a whole, the order of the Beatitudes seems very intentional. Consider the following:

1) *Poverty of spirit* ⇨ *mourning* ⇨ *meekness* – all qualities of the heart and spirit, assuming related actions, and *prerequisites for a right relationship with God*

2) ⇨ *A strong desire for righteousness* (i.e., a consistent hunger for being right with God and for doing what is right) ⇨ *mercy* (i.e., being right and acting right with people and with creation – a result of first being right with God) ⇨ *purity* (being right with yourself and your conscience, single-mindedness)—all three of which, following on from the first three, are *prerequisites for service to God and people*

3) *Peacemaking,* the *practical result of the qualities of heart and preparation for service*

4) ⇨ *Persecution* – the *natural result of doing what is right and standing for what is right*

To reverse the order would go against what, I believe, Jesus was teaching here.

And then there are the *results* of each:

1) *The kingdom of heaven now near and accessible* ⇨ *comfort, joy* ⇨ *inheritance,* all *results of a right relationship with God*

2) ⇨ *A filling-up with the blessings of God and with righteousness* ⇨ *experience of mercy coming from God and others* ⇨ *"seeing God" (singlemindedness bringing clarity of vision and purpose), the result of service to God and people*

3) *Being called "the children of God", a favour from God (He calls us His children), perhaps also recognition from others that we are God's children (obviously not from all since we see what comes next)*

4) ⇨ *Persecution, though with joy and reward—the natural result of doing right. The last is not about a quality as much as an experience, a result of all that has come before*

The passage *starts* with poverty of spirit and mourning, but *ends* with rejoicing, "excessive or ecstatic joy and delight", (Strong), and heavenly reward. It's a positive progression, though with a certain amount of discomfort at the beginning since mourning is not enjoyable when it's happening; and at the end since persecution can also be trying, although by the time we get there we are, or perhaps should be, able to rejoice and be "exceeding glad" about it!

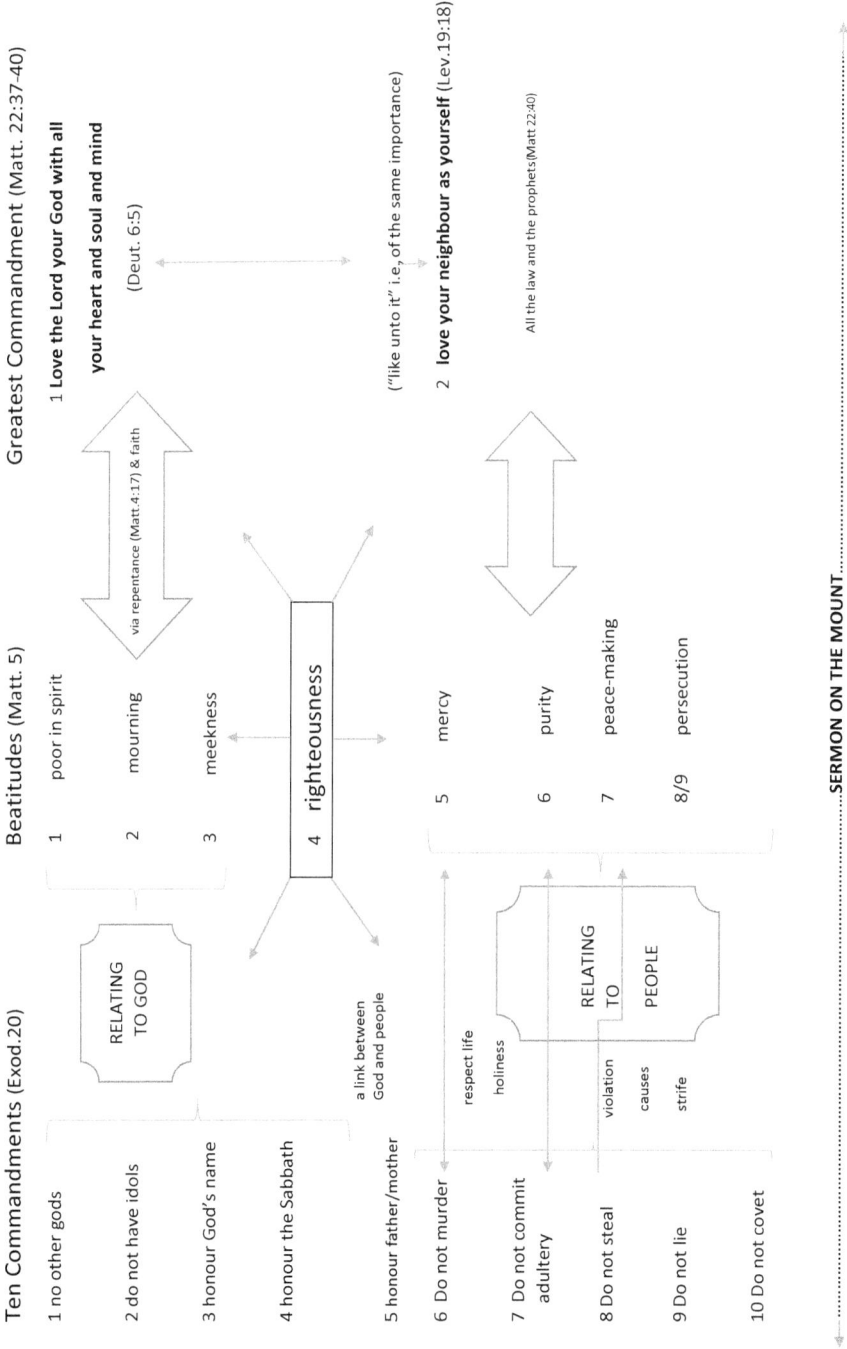

Ten Commandments (Exod.20)　　Beatitudes (Matt. 5)　　Greatest Commandment (Matt. 22:37-40)

1 Love the Lord your God with all

your heart and soul and mind

(Deut. 6:5)

("like unto it" i.e, of the same importance)

2 love your neighbour as yourself (Lev.19:18)

All the law and the prophets(Matt 22:40)

via repentance (Matt 4:17) & faith

1　poor in spirit

2　mourning

3　meekness

4　righteousness

5　mercy

6　purity

7　peace-making

8/9　persecution

RELATING
TO GOD

a link between
God and people

RELATING
TO
PEOPLE

respect life

holiness

violation

causes

strife

1 no other gods

2 do not have idols

3 honour God's name

4 honour the Sabbath

5 honour father/mother

6 Do not murder

7 Do not commit
adultery

8 Do not steal

9 Do not lie

10 Do not covet

SERMON ON THE MOUNT

BIBLIOGRAPHY

Barclay, W. (1964). *New Testament Words.* Philadelphia: The Westminster Press.

Barclay, W. (1975). *The Daily Study Bible The Gospel of Luke.* Edinburgh: The Saint Andrew Press.

Flynn, L. B. (1987). *The Twelve.* Wheaton, Illinois: Victor Books.

Howley, G. C. D. (Gen.Ed). (1969). *A New Testament Commentary.* London: Pickering & Inglis Ltd.

Strong, J. (1990). *The New Strong's Exhaustive Concordance of the Bible.* Nashville, Tennessee: Thomas Nelson Publishers.

Vine, W. E. (1952). *An Expository Dictionary of New Testament Words.* Iowa Falls: Riverside Book and Bible House.

Voice of the Martyrs. (Jan/Feb 2010). *Reaching out to a tortured nation - Madness and Metal Walls,* 3.

Wuest, K. S. (1945). *Bypaths in the Greek New Testament.* Grand Rapids, Michigan: W.M.B.Eerdmans Publishing Co.

ALSO AVAILABLE

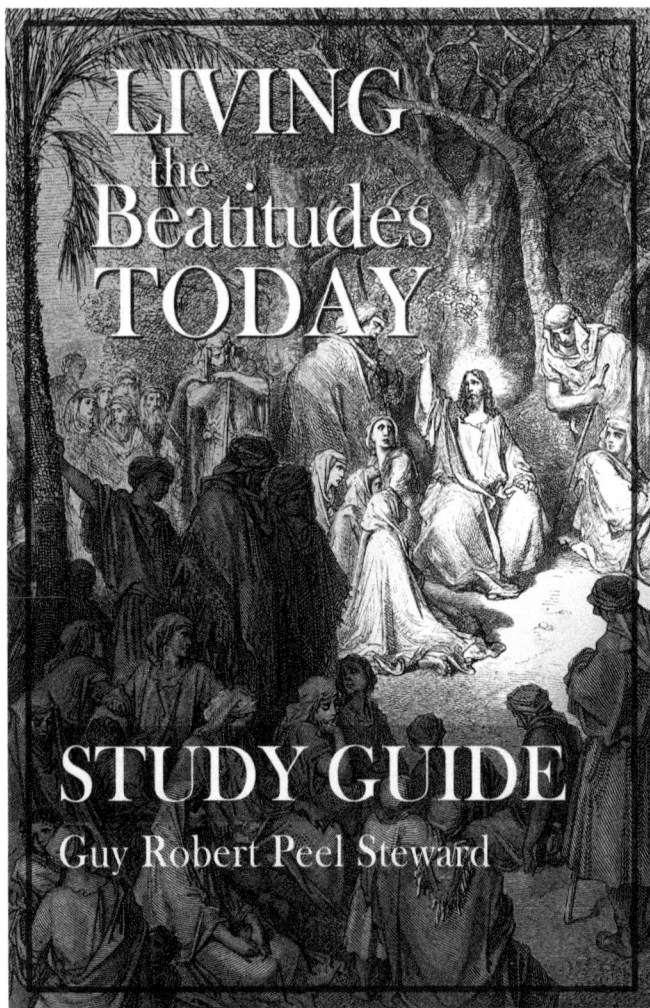

LIVING the Beatitudes TODAY

STUDY GUIDE

Guy Robert Peel Steward

For more information about

Guy Robert Peel Steward
and
Living the Beatitudes Today
please visit:

www.guysteward.com

Ambassador International's mission is to magnify the Lord Jesus Christ and promote His gospel through the written word.

We believe through the publication of Christian literature, Jesus Christ and His Word will be exalted, believers will be strengthened in their walk with Him, and the lost will be directed to Jesus Christ as the only way of salvation.

For more information about
AMBASSADOR INTERNATIONAL
please visit:

www.ambassador-international.com
@AmbassadorIntl
www.facebook.com/AmbassadorIntl

Thank you for reading this book. Please consider leaving us a review on your social media, favorite retailer's website, Goodreads or Bookbub, or our website.

www.ingramcontent.com/pod-product-compliance
Lightning Source LLC
LaVergne TN
LVHW021612080426
835510LV00019B/2533

Living the Beatitudes Today looks at the basic building blocks of the Christian life – found in Jesus's first recorded sermon — and unveils how they act like a hinge between the Old and New Covenants, encapsulating the law of Moses, the messages of the prophets, plus the teachings of Jesus and of all the New Testament.

Living the Beatitudes Today reveals the power of the two greatest commandments and of the golden rule. It examines the clear theological and practical implications of the Beatitudes for the believer in Christ, challenges the wrong assumptions about the Beatitudes, and invites the seeker to step out on a journey, through an understanding of the Beatitudes, towards a lifetime of ever-increasing connection with their Creator, and to truly live the Beatitudes today.

Guy Steward was educated at King's School, King's College, and Selwyn College in Auckland, NZ. During much of his twenties, he ran a small business. He holds a BA with a music major, and a BTh from New Covenant International Theological Seminary through its associate, NCI Bible college in New Zealand, and he also has a teaching diploma from the Auckland College of Education. Guy has taught both Music and English at New Zealand high schools. He is currently teaching English and Art History at a foundation course preparing students for university. He lives in Auckland with his wife and son. Amongst other church ministries, Guy has been involved in men's ministry, and, with his wife, as a cell group leader.

RELIGION | Christian Living | Spiritual Growth
RELIGION|Bible Studies|New Testament|Jesus, the Gospels, & Acts

US $13.99|UK £9.99|$17.99 CAD|$18.99 AUD|$19.99 NZD

ISBN 978-1-64960-036-3

51399 >

EAN

9 781649 600363

Ambassador International
GREENVILLE, SOUTH CAROLINA & BELFAST, NORTHERN IRELAND

www.ambassador-international.com

Magnifying Jesus while promoting His gospel through the written word.